Into the Valley

Marines at Guadalcanal

John Hersey

ILLUSTRATED BY COL. DONALD L. DICKSON, USMCR

University of Nebraska Press
Lincoln and London

Foreword

The first postulate of the theorem of war is death. The problem set by the theorem for a writer about World War II—in particular for a war correspondent, writing soon after an action on the basis of raw experience—was how to arrive at the "truth" about warfare.

The key word in that last sentence is in quotation marks because, as Tolstoy made clear in *War and Peace,* there are as many truths about a given battle, after it, as there were participants in it. The correspondent was only one of them—and a peripheral one, at that, since the military discipline under which he operated was polluted by the fact that he got his actual marching orders from a publication. The correspondent's "truths" in what he wrote were purely subjective, filtered through his eyes and ears, conditioned by his temperament, by the particular culture in which he had been bred, by the pressure of the policies of his employer, and above all by his groping sense of the meaning of his own life in the harsh circumstances in which he found himself.

The meaning of his life was, for him, the positive value in the theorem. Its negative reciprocal, the threat of a death that might seem meaningless, was a constant, always there, nagging him like a third-degree interrogation, goading him with selfish fear, challenging him to be responsible and "brave" and to use words carefully, but also causing him, while in actual battle, to keep a sharp eye at all times on something that was not available to the footsoldier beside him: the nearest exit. We will see in this book how some Marines ran for such a getaway but were barred from it by their commanding officer. The correspondent could take it. His duty was to write his story—which conveniently meant that he must make every effort to save his own life, in order to be able to send off his copy.

In this foreword I shall do my best to recall, from nearly half a century away, the process by which a callow young journalist became a war correspondent in the first place, and how, very early in his playing of that role, he came to write about his descent into the valley of the shadow of death on Guadalcanal. My hope is that in this roundabout way I can help a reader to parse some of the "truths"—and falsehoods—in this book.

The story began late on Sunday afternoon, 7 December 1941, on the twenty-ninth floor of the Time & Life Building, in Rockefeller Center, New York, when the wire-service teletype machine in its secluded little room began uttering an urgent thumping that could be heard all up and down the halls. I was then writing *Time*'s coverage of the war in Europe. The magazine went to press on each Monday night, so Sunday was the busiest writing day of the week. I don't remember who first checked the machine, but I know I was soon summoned to read its appalling message: Pearl Harbor had been attacked by the Japanese, and our Pacific battleship fleet was a shambles.

This news changed everything. An American journalist was no longer an observer of war; he was at war. It seemed to me that the Pacific conflict would be for the most part a sea war, and I soon applied for a commission in the Navy. The paperwork on my application was fairly far along when, one day, Dan Longwell, the executive editor of *Life,* appeared in my office and urged me to give up the idea of joining a service and, instead, let Time Incorporated apply for a military exemption for me as a war correspondent. He put it to me that I could do more for my country in this way than by joining the Navy, using my explicit training as a journalist for the public good. The unspoken subtext of this high-minded appeal, it goes without saying, was that I could do more in this way for *Time* and *Life*.

After a few days, I accepted the suggestion. And soon after that, having read about the Japanese sinking of the British battle cruiser *Repulse,* in a harrowing account by Cecil Brown, the CBS correspondent in Singapore who, along with O'Dowd Gallagher of the London *Daily Express,* had barely survived the disaster, I began to live with a vivid realization that the public and corporate good that Longwell had urged me to serve might cost me my life. This was no more dire or honorable a prospect, I hasten to say, than that of a soldier or sailor; I simply mean that the possibility came home to me. Through the depressing months of the spring, while I waited to be cleared to go to the Pacific, the Japanese inflicted one humiliation after another on the Allies, and added one increment after another to my anxiety: at Manila, Hong Kong, the Malay Peninsula, Bataan, Wake, Thailand, Guam.

By early summer I was in uniform and on my way, borne on a tide of servicemen going out to action. San Francisco was the jumping-off place. It did not take much acuity to understand that although fear of death was never mentioned, it was universally shared, and that the way of dealing with it was to eat, drink, have sex if possible, and be very merry. A primary focus of blustering seemed to be the Top of the Mark, in the penthouse of the Mark Hopkins Hotel at the crest of Nob Hill, with its bar and its dimmed lights and its breathtaking view westward of the sparkling city and, beyond, of a mysterious darkness where the sea of the war began its reach.

In Honolulu, with the stark wreckage of Pearl Harbor all too visible nearby, I encountered the same urgent energy of everyone's last fling. Waiting for orders, I was housed in a tiny cottage of the Halekulani Hotel, right on Waikiki Beach. It was handily near the Moana, which turned out to be the headquarters of abandon. I soon met up with a fellow correspondent for *Time* and *Life*, Bill Chickering, who was also on his way out (to death at sea, as it turned out, in the Battle of Lingayen Gulf, off Luzon). Bill got me together with some high-living Navy divebomber pilots, who proposed that we all fly over to make the acquaintance of a famously lovely and loving redheaded nurse at a naval air station on the island of Maui. So we did, in a covey of open-cockpit Navy Dauntless divebombing planes. The nurse was indeed lovely, though to tell the objective truth she was very slightly cross-eyed. On the way back, the pilot with whom I was flying—I've forgotten his name—decided in the desperate extremity of his hangover to dive straight down from high in the sky into the oblivion of a ravishing waterfall that tumbled down the sheer cliffs of the windward face of Molokai. He pulled out and up at the last moment. This was the first time I didn't die in the Pacific.

Journalism was not so much then, as it has since become, the adversary ferret of errors of judgment in those who govern and command, and the Navy's authorities accordingly granted their accredited journalists an amazing degree of trust. With other correspondents I was summoned to a briefing at Pearl Harbor. After many reversals, our side had recently achieved its first victory. On 4 June, off the island of Midway, at a cost of one aircraft carrier and 150 planes, our carrier- and land-based aircraft had sunk four Japanese carriers and a heavy cruiser and destroyed 253 planes. We were now told that United States forces were preparing to move from a purely defensive posture to a defensive-offensive one. Our intelligence having broken the Japanese codes, it had been learned that the Japanese were building an airfield on Guadalcanal Island—a potential threat to Allied supply lines from Hawaii to the South Pacific. We correspondents were openly told, with appropriate cautions about security, that the U.S. First Marine Division, then in New Zealand, would attack Guadalcanal about two weeks later.

I promptly submitted to the Navy censor a radio message for my editor at *Time*: "If you are a wise man, you will know what to put on the cover of the first issue in August." Guadalcanal was in the Solomon Islands; Solomon was wise. The censor—either he didn't get the point or he thought the Japanese, if they intercepted it, wouldn't—passed the message, and it went off. *Time* did get the point and had a timely cover story.

My assignment now came through: I boarded the carrier *Hornet,* which, on 17 August, ten days after the Marines landed on Guadalcanal, set sail for the far South Pacific, to help guard the supply lines for the precarious beachhead in the Solomons. On the trip out, a sweet, safe voyage on a lapis-lazuli sea, the shoreside atmosphere of merriment prevailed, so far as it could without the help of booze and women. Games of poker, rolling of dice, tall tales, practical jokes, awful singing. When we crossed the equator there was an elaborate, prank-filled ceremony, of a sort that I suppose the disenchanted, streetwise servicemen of post-Vietnam America would today consider ridiculously namby-pamby. High-ranking officers dressed themselves up as Father Neptune and his fishy courtiers; poetry that had been scribbled in the officers' mess was read over a loudspeaker; those who had never crossed the line were put through hoops of initiation, being assigned bizarre tasks and paying slapstick penalties for failure in them. The whole affair was like a birthday party for twelve-year-old boys; it was as if, for one afternoon, those grown men on their way to the zone of death needed to pay a cleansing farewell visit to childhood.

In due course the *Hornet* joined a sister carrier, the *Wasp*, in a task force comprising, besides those two ships, a couple of cruisers and a bevy of destroyers, and these vessels paraded in formation back and forth, back and forth, in the waters south of New Caledonia, the New Hebrides, and the Solomons, the carriers repeatedly launching their aircraft in searches for signs of the enemy. The *Hornet* seemed a floating city. The company was congenial; I stood many happy watches in our battle station on the lofty signal bridge with the artist-writer Tom Lea. We seemed to be on a luxury cruise in tropical waters. I made lots of friends. Danger was in hiding.

From a professional point of view, however, the duty was frustrating. There were no stories to write. Nothing happened. The weather was perfect. Tom and I could look down at the flying bridge and see the admiral in charge of the task force poking with his little finger at a fungus infection he had in his ear. What was he waiting for? Why didn't he—or his superiors—order us up closer to the notorious "slot" of the Solomons, through which the Japanese kept feeding reinforcements to harass the beleaguered Marines on Guadalcanal?

Then something bad did happen. On the serene and breathless afternoon of the fifteenth of September, not far from us on the glassy sea, the *Wasp* was hit by torpedoes. We watched, horrified, as the ship was shaken by a series of internal explosions, and a slanting fan of black smoke rose, and the ship listed, fatally crippled. We learned that night that our own forces had sunk the derelict. Some of her planes had managed to escape to fields on New Caledonia and Espíritu Santo.

A few days later the *Hornet* put into Nouméa, on the French island of New Caledonia, to reprovision. Both Tom Lea and I went ashore and got permission to leave the ship. (A bit more than a month later, on 27 October, the *Hornet* was sunk in the Battle of Santa Cruz. An enemy *kamikaze* divebombed directly onto the signal bridge, where Tom and I would have been standing had we remained aboard—for me, another evasion of death in the Pacific Theater.) An officer in Nouméa cut orders for me to go north to Guadalcanal, and in a few days I was able to hitch a ride there on a supply plane.

Henderson Field on Guadalcanal, begun by the Japanese, was in a coconut plantation on a coastal plain near Lunga Point. Its runway glistened as we circled to land, for by now it was surfaced with a long strip of Marston matting, a steel mesh rolled out in lengthwise segments on a base of crushed coral, to give planes a more or less smooth surface for landings and takeoffs. Soon after I deplaned with my bedroll and gear, I made my way to the pilots' ready tent beside the field, and there I recognized, from behind him, a friend named Alfred Wright, who had been a fellow writer on *Time*. He was a flier in the *Wasp* group, which had been sent in after the sinking to support the Marines. He was reading as I came up behind him, and I saw over his shoulder that his book was a Modem Library edition of Freud's *Introduction to Psychoanalysis. His* first words to me, holding up the book, were, "I'm ready for some of this." (It was true. A few days later he had to be evacuated, because on night missions, flying along on the level, he would suddenly become convinced that his plane was nosing over in an out-of-control dive.)

He was not the only one on the raw edge, as I soon saw. The Marines' combat task was supposed to be to carry out an initial assault, and when they had secured a landing they were supposed to be relieved by Army troops trained and equipped to hold and expand a beachhead. But now for almost two months, through ferocious attack after attack by the relentless Japanese, by land, by sea, and by air, the landing force had had to fight on. They got little sleep. At night naval vessels bombarded the beachhead, or a single big twin-engine flying boat—called "Washing Machine Charley" by the defenders because its unsynchronized engines ground along with an irregular beat—kept thrumming up and down all night, dropping a random bomb from time to time. A week or so before I got there, the beachhead had sustained a twenty-four-hour naval shelling, and then a nightmarish two-day firefight had taken place that came to be called the Battle of Bloody Ridge, in which the enemy, as it poured wave after suicidal wave on the Marines' positions, resorted to nerve-wracking tricks. They would talk loudly, drawing fire that told them the defenders' positions. They released smoke and shouted, in English, "Gas attack! Gas attack!" They screamed obscentities as they charged. They issued commands and fake reports on the Marines' radio wavelengths. They broke the beachhead perimeter and reached nearly to the division command post. The Marines' managed to turn the tide, but even when obviously defeated the Japanese kept coming. They went so far as to stage a hopeless bayonet attack in broad daylight.

There had been a series of equally terrible battles before that one. Exhausted, given no hope of relief, losing close friends, familiar with the stench of the enemy dead, the Marines had held on through weeks of torment such as few soldiers in all history had suffered. On top of everything else, they began coming down with jungle diseases: dysentery, malaria, dengue, a kind of typhus called tsutsugamushi disease, "foot rot," and the horrible "crud" of fungus.

What struck me above all, in the comparative lull of my first days on the island, was the eerie normalcy of the behavior of the Marines and navy fliers, haggard and spent as they were. It was as if, even here where death was part of the normalcy, they could push it away with good cheer. Games of poker, rolling of dice, tall tales, practical jokes, awful singing. "I am having fun," Captain Rigaud, who was to lead me into the valley, wrote in one of his letters home that his family let me read on my return to the States. I was invited one night during the lull, while Washing Machine Charley droned overhead, to a party in a certain Marine tent. When I arrived, a few men were seated in a circle on the ground; at the center of the circle was a lit lantern and a bottle of cheap bourbon called Green River. You could tell whether the hosts liked whoever lifted the tent flap. If they disliked him, they would say, "Sit down, have a drink," and they would pass him the visible Green River, but if they liked him, they would say, "Sit down and shut up," and soon they would pass around, behind their backs, out of the light, a bottle of much better Old Granddad. God knows how the liquor had reached them.

One afternoon I learned that a flier who had been shot down over the sea had drifted ashore in an inflatable raft and had been given sanctuary by a Catholic mission at the southeastern tip of the island, out of the area of combat. A rescue flight of two unbelievably ancient planes—Grumman "Ducks," two-seater open-cockpit amphibious biplanes that looked as if they had been used in World War I—was going down to pick him up. I asked permission to ride along. As it turned out, I got much more story than I wanted that afternoon, for it brought the third and fourth times I didn't die in the Pacific. I tell the story because it sharply affected the mindset I carried down into the valley a few days later.

My pilot was a young boy named Cherry, who told me he had had only forty hours' flying time. I was strapped into a parachute and a safety belt, and we took off. The parachute wouldn't have done much good; we flew through rain squalls at about a hundred feet above the jungle. We landed in calm water off a tiny bay. As we taxied in, we suddenly came up on a shallow reef, and Cherry prudently put the plane's wheels down so that the pontoon would not be torn up on the jagged coral. We got off somehow; he raised the wheels and found a channel into the bay, where we were greeted by two English priests, the survivor, and several cheerful natives.

It was decided that the survivor would go back to Henderson Field in the rear seat of the other plane, and Cherry and I took off. Right after we cleared the water, there was a mysterious thump from the Duck's undercarriage. Cherry circled, trying to make out what had happened. I saw the group on the ground waving wildly, and shouted to Cherry. He decided to land in the bay again, to see what the trouble was.

The moment we touched the water, the little plane lurched, flipped over in a sickening forward somersault, and began to sink. I found myself upside down, eight or ten feet underwater, perhaps going deeper and deeper, and strapped tight in my seat. Somehow I managed to unbuckle the chute and belt, pushed myself down and out of the cockpit, and swam up toward the light, my lungs bursting. I reached air just as my vision began to blur. The first thing I saw, when my eyes cleared, was my small field notebook floating in front of me; I had sheathed it in a condom (a number of which perhaps I should explain, I had bought in the ship's store on the *Hornet* for this very purpose—to keep notebooks dry). About two feet of the upside-down pontoon still loomed above the surface. I dived down to see if I could rescue Cherry. It turned out that he had come up on other side of the pontoon and was diving down to rescue me. We finally heard each other splashing. Soon two of the natives came out in a dugout canoe and took us ashore, and we learned what had happened. Apparently the lift mechanism of the right-hand wheel had become clogged with a clump of living coral or seaweed out on the reef, and it had dropped into its down position after our takeoff—and had tripped the plane when we landed again.

The pilot of the other plane offered to take me back to the beachhead if I would be willing to lie prone in the pontoon, which the missionaries had already crammed with melons and fresh vegetables from their gardens. Cherry could be picked up later. On the flight back, cradled in produce, I could see nothing. I could hear through the roar and vibrations of the engine the sounds of a thunderstorm. I felt the thud of the wheels touching down. Then, as the pilot put his brakes on, came the awful sounds of a skid on the slick wet Marston matting. The plane swerved off the runway and crashed in the bordering jungle. The plane was totaled, but the two fliers were unhurt and I got out with nothing worse than a broken rib (which wasn't diagnosed until quite a bit later). Mission accomplished: two planes, but no lives, lost.

The fifth time I didn't die in the Pacific was on 8 October, when I went into the valley.

After the battle there I returned to the beachhead, drained to the last drop. The pain on the left side of my ribcage, which I had been able to push out of my mind in the novelty and turmoil of the action, was now severe. I bathed the next afternoon in the Lunga River, and found that I already had a bad case of foot rot—ugly pustules around my ankles. Medics gave me sulfa powder to treat them. I spent several days going over my notes, checking names and details, and filling out the story of the death of the man named Bauer. And then, with my chest pain worsening, I was advised to ship out and go home—counsel that I was all too willing to follow.

It took nearly two weeks to hitch rides to New York. I went at once to Oriskany Falls, upstate, to gather background on Captain Rigaud, and then I wrote an article for Life about his company's skirmish. After that the broken rib was diagnosed, and I was given a week's leave, during which I wrote this book in bed.

Did I write the truth about what happened in the valley? This question fascinates and troubles me, nearly five decades later. I believe, reading now what I wrote then, after my first experience of warfare, that it is partly true to what happened, and partly not.

An essential truth that I recorded, which probably had some value for homeside readers at that uneasy stage of the Pacific war—and may have some value today—was that Americans are not invincible. I had witnessed defeat, panic, flight. There had come a moment when the imminence of death simply overpowered a group of men, even though they were members of a hyper-proud service, were well trained, and were veterans of terrible battles that had proven them brave.

The quality of bravery is complex; courage earns a red badge for its mystery. A key passage in this book brought into common usage in the language a phrase that sometimes came to be spoken derisively: our men were "fighting for apple pie." The passage, as you will see, was an account of a conversation on the field of battle that would not have taken place but for the intrusive curiosity of a journalist. (The mere presence of a correspondent on the field, with his pencil and notebook in evidence, was bound to contaminate the natural unfolding of truth.) When I asked a group of intelligent officers what they thought they were fighting for, in that valley, they went vague before they spoke— got a look on their faces of "men bothered by a memory." I think that their oblique answers were, for them, almost unbearably truthful, even though their words raised troubling questions about courage and about American war aims.

Folk tongues have long spoken of "pie in the sky" as yearned-for happiness; these men wanted with all their hearts to get the damn thing over and go home—to pie, among other things. I still think it was deeply true, as I wrote in the book, that if before the action "some lieutenant colonel had come up and given them their choice between going into the valley and going home, they would have said the hell with the valley." This seems to me a much more rational and mature response to warfare than that of highly motivated ideologues, who would, like automatons, declare for the other choice. (Bear in mind that we have some ideologues in the United States.)

If you ask how a nation could win a war whose soldiers would opt for apple pie rather than a chance for heroic death, I would be inclined to answer that this is one of the main reasons why our side won. There was a lifesaving skepticism and irony embedded in the confused courage of men bred to free choice. Nearly three years later, doing an article on the elite U.S. Army Ranger Battalion, I ran across the case of a soldier in cruel fighting in Italy who showed such signs of fear that his commanding officer, who expected blind courage from his men, asked what the devil he was so agitated about. "I ain't afraid," the soldier answered. "I'm just shaking with patriotism." The fanatical *banzai* attacks and the suicidal *kamikaze* dives failed, in the end, and so did Hitler's true believers, and that ironic, trembling GI turned out to be on the winning side. I need hardly point out that no lieutenant colonel showed up on Guadalcanal, that afternoon, to offer the men a choice, and the company did go into the valley.

One statement I made in this book now seems to me to have been of doubtful truth: "Courage is largely the desire to show other men that you have it." In a proud corps like the Marines, there would indeed be some pressure to show your mettle to your friends. But it is clear that what we think of as "courage" can range all the way from pure self-sacrifice for the sake of others to the release of a deep and gross bloodlust; it could embrace the cool steadfastness of David facing Goliath with his slingshot, the costly sulking anger of Achilles, the implicit love of others of Horatio at the bridge, the idiotic fervor of the men of the Light Brigade—and, alas, the telegenic viciousness, so popular in recent years with violence-besotted American viewers, of a Rambo. On the *Hornet* I made the acquaintance of—and took many notes on—a flier who, years later, became the model for a novel set in another theater of war and entitled, in honor of his grotesque form of courage, *The War Lover.*

One of several half-truths in the book is my claim that being green that afternoon and not knowing what to expect "kept me from being afraid." Some weeks after the skirmish in the valley, I received from Secretary of the Navy Frank Knox a letter of commendation for my bravery in helping to evacuate the wounded from the field of battle. I should have sent it back. My alacrity in helping to get the wounded out was my way of taking the quickest possible exit from that hellhole. I had been so frightened by my near-drowning when Cherry's plane flipped over, and by thinking about it afterward, that I believe I had very nearly plumbed the depths of my capacity for fear, and in the valley, as a consequence, I was really in a kind of daze, a frightful state of being stupidly rattled—with my "duty" as a war correspondent offering me just enough distraction to keep me more or less functional. It may also be that, five times spared death, I was beginning to have an illusion—or delusion—that it would never be able to reach me.

There are a number of minor untruths, stated or implied, in, this book, of which I will give a couple of examples.

At one point I speak of the Geneva Convention, under which correspondents, though assigned a so-called "assimilated rank" of first lieutenant, were classified as noncombatants and were not supposed to carry arms. The passage is written very carefully, so that I never actually assert that I was unarmed, but the suggestion is certainly there. In fact, just before we descended into the valley, one of the headquarters officers gave me an automatic pistol to take with me. In a figurative sense, what I wrote was true enough because in my untrained hands the gun was more a talisman than a weapon.

You will see that throughout the book I put in the mouths of Marines such words as "gollydingwhiz," "damn," "hell," "gosh," and "dung." More stringent, in those days, than the Geneva Convention was the convention, in using printed words, of self-censorship in order to make publication possible. The truth is that strong words, then unprintable, were so frequently on the tongues of servicemen that they had lost their tang and punch; totally worn out, four-letter words came to mean no more than three-letter words like "and" and "the." After dark, one night, I hitched a ride in a jeep around the perimeter of

Henderson Field. The enlisted driver, obeying regulations, was poking along very slowly with his lights out. A jeep came in the opposite direction with headlights blazing. As we passed, my driver shouted to the other one, "Turn your fucking lights out!" The other driver called back, "I can't. I've got the fucking colonel with me."

From this distance, I am very troubled by the dialogue in the book. I did take notes in the valley, awkwardly tucking the pistol under an armpit and writing shaky words, but the dialogue had to be rounded out and reconstructed in New York a month later. This technique came to be commonplace among the so-called New Journalists from the sixties onward, and I learned to deplore it and to try to avoid it. It is one thing for a journalist to record speech on tape or put it down immediately after an interview from full notes; it is another to reinvent it much later for use in what purports to be a factual account or in a nonfiction novel (an oxymoron, if there ever was one). For most journalists the temptation to improve is too great, and the end result is that the "truth" of the work is compromised further than it was already bound to be by the subjective eye and ear and writing "voice" of the journalist. The trouble with the publication, over and over again, of improved and shaded and jazzed-up "truths" is that eventually a dulled public can't tell the difference between real facts and barefaced lies. For example: in a presidential campaign—where truth can be presumed to matter.

I have resisted the strong temptation to revise *Into the Valley* for this edition. The first passages to be cut would have been those that refer to the Japanese as animals. It was all very well—and "truthful" enough, for such things were indeed being said—for me to quote a Marine as wishing he were fighting against (white, blond?) Germans, who "react like men," instead of against these Japanese animals, who "take to the jungle as if they had been bred there." But to my shame I am not quoting someone else when, after the mortar barrage begins, I write that I envisage "a swarm of intelligent little animals" fussing around the mortar tubes on the other side of the river.

What can I say? I confess that I had grown up with an anti-Japanese bias. I had been born and had spent my childhood in China, whose people believe that the ancient Japanese stole and corrupted their culture. In 1937, as a grownup back in the States, I had been horrified, in my sympathy for the Chinese, by accounts and pictures of the orgiastic Japanese rape of Nanking. I had visited North China as a journalist in 1939, and had seen with my own eyes the arrogance and cruelty of the Japanese occupation of the city where I was born. Like other Americans, I had reacted badly to the humiliations of Pearl Harbor and Bataan. And now on Guadalcanal the Japanese skill and American discomfort in jungle warfare were all too vivid in my mind. . . . All of which may explain but does not justify what I wrote.

War is, among other things, a school, and during the rest of World War II, I learned some lessons that radically changed my views. One of the things I learned was that war makes no national or racial or ideological distinctions as it degrades human beings. I learned of my country's incarceration, on racial grounds alone, and in contravention of our most honored civil rights, of Japanese-American citizens (some of whom had sons and brothers in the American army) in concentration camps. I covered the fighting against the Germans in Sicily—during the course of which I witnessed the arrogance and cruelty of a revered American general. In Sicily my life was spared, twice more, in two harrowing airplane accidents—and again on successive flights; my sense of the value of my own life, and therefore of that of others, was intensified. I flew on the first bombing raid on Rome and from then on could visualize, from the deliverers' point of view, the wanton savagery of air attacks on civilians. On conducted tours from the Soviet Union I talked with survivors of Nazi massacres at concentration camps near Tallinn, Estonia, and at Radogocz, Poland. I saw the ruins of the Warsaw ghetto and met survivors, liberated only ten days earlier, of the Lodz ghetto, some of whom kissed my hand, not because I was an American but because I was a journalist and could tell, tell, tell. Later on, I saw the miles of appalling ruins of Tokyo caused by myriad fire-bombs—and the apocalyptic devastation of Hiroshima caused by a single bomb dropped from a lone American plane.

All these experiences brought me to some "truths"—as I saw them—about warfare. It was clear that we had had to fight that war, even though its axiom of death had made us set aside one of the most awesome and precious taboos of our Judeo-Christian heritage: Thou shalt not kill. We had had no choice. Japanese militarism and the plague of Hitler's insanity threatened not only our physical security but also the moral underpinnings of Western civilization. But I had also come to realize that if our concept of that civilization was to mean anything, we had to acknowledge the humanity of even our misled and murderous enemies. What argued against cutting shameful words from this book for a new edition was that having them appear there, today, nearly half a century later, might help to show what warfare could do to a young mind that thought it was in pursuit of truth.

—John Hersey
April 1989

INTO THE VALLEY

Marines at Guadalcanal

On the eighth day of October in the first year of our war, I went down into a valley with Captain Charles Rigaud of the United States Marines. A small skirmish took place down there.

The valley was on Guadalcanal Island, but it might have been anywhere.

The skirmish was just an episode in an insignificant battle. The whole battle, which lasted three days, did not bring as much reward to our arms as several other battles on that island and elsewhere have done.

But the battle, and especially the skirmish with Rigaud, illustrated how war feels to men everywhere. The terrain, the weapons and the races of war vary, but certainly never the sensations, except in degree, for they are as universal as those of love.

This book is an attempt to recapture the feelings of Rigaud, his men, and myself, when we went into that jungle valley. If people in the homes could feel those feelings for an hour, or even just know about them, I think we would be an inch or two closer to winning the war and trying like hell to make the peace permanent.

The characters of this book all are or were real men, and any resemblance to characters of fiction is purely coincidental. In order to spare the feelings of next of kin, I have changed the names of three men—the ones who are called in this book Utley, Bauer and O'Brien.

Rigaud's skirmish came on the second day of the battle, so I shall briefly give the background as I saw it.

The action was called the Third Battle of the Matanikau River. Few Americans have ever heard of the Matanikau River, to say nothing of its Third Battle. The river is a light brown stream winding through a jungle valley about five miles west of Henderson Field. When I arrived on Guadalcanal, our forces did not hold positions out to the Matanikau. The Japs were moving up in some strength, evidently to try to establish their bridgehead—the first in a series of heavy moves against our camp. It became imperative for our troops to push to the river and force the enemy back beyond it, before it was too late.

The first two battles of the Matanikau River had been earlier attempts to do just that. In the first one, the Marines tried to do the job frontally, but their force was too small. In the second, they tried a tactic of encirclement, but again not enough men were thrown into action. This third time, with the enemy constantly growing in strength, there could be no question of failing. . . .

"Awright! Reveille! It's six o'clock. Come on, fellas, all out. Reveille!"

Although it was just barely light, it did not take much persuasion to start the men in Colonel Amor Leroy Sims's camp stirring. They wandered out to brush their teeth, to shave, to start cramming things into their packs, to polish their already polished rifles.

Word was passed up through the encampment: "Mass at six-thirty for those who want it. Six-thirty mass." Attendance was pretty good that morning. While that religious rite was being carried out, there was also a pagan touch. Four buzzards flew over the camp. "To the right hand," said a young marine, like a Roman sage. "Our fortunes will be good."

One of the last orders we had heard Colonel Sims give the evening before was to the officer of the mess: "Breakfast in the morning must be a good, solid, hot meal. And if we get back from starving ourselves for two or three days out there and find that you fellows who stay behind have been gourmandizing, someone'll be shot at dawn."

Breakfast was solid, all right—our last square meal for three days. On the table there were huge pans full of sliced pineapples, beans, creamed chipped beef, a rice-and-raisin stew, crackers, canned butter, jam and coffee.

As the units began lining up to move out, the first artillery barrage broke out—75's and 105's coughing deeply, and then a minute later the answering coughs, far out. At 8:30 the column started to move. We had a good long hike ahead of us. Colonel Sims's encampment was about eight miles from the Matanikau, but terrain would force the column to move at least fifteen miles before contact.

The first sensation when we began to move against the enemy was one of great elation. In the marines, this came out as boasting.

"We're not so dumb," one said. "We don't own this lousy island, and we don't want to own it, never. All we want is to knock the hell out of these Japs."

Another said: "And we will, you can bet your shirt we will."

A third chimed in: "When you get a little farther out, you'll begin to smell the dead Japs we've left up in the trees and on the ridges."

Gradually the column fell into silence. The walking, which had been casual and purposely out of step, began to get stiffer and more formal, and finally much of the column was in step. On the engineers' crudely bull-dozed roadway, there began to be a regular *crunch-crunch-crunch* that reminded me of all the newsreels I had seen of feet parading on asphalt, to a background of cheering and band music. As a matter of fact we had a band with us, but the bandsmen were equipped with first-aid stuff, stretchers and rifles.

For a time the column wound through thick jungle, then emerged on a grassy plain edged by a kind of Great Wall of steep, bare ridges. Just before we reached the first of the ridges, Colonel Sims turned in his position at the head of the column and said: "Ten minute break. Get off the road, spread right out."

Lieutenant Colonel Julian Frisbie, Colonel Sims's hulking executive officer, sat cross-legged in the grass and thundered at me: "Would you like to hear about our plan of operation?"

"It is a very simple scheme," he explained. "We know that the Japs have moved up into positions on the other side of the mouth of the Matanikau. Perhaps some of them have already crossed to this side. Our aim is to cut off and kill or capture as many as we can. Those which we don't pocket we must drive back.

"Edson—that's Colonel Merritt Edson, who trained the first Marine raiders—will push a holding attack to the river right at its mouth, and try to make the Japs think that we intend to force a crossing there. Whaling actually will force a crossing quite a little higher up, and then will wheel downstream beside the river. Hanneken will lead part of our force through behind Whaling, will go deeper than Whaling, and then cut right. Then Puller will go through deeper yet and cut right too. If necessary another force will go around by sea in Higgins boats and land behind the Japs to close the trap.

"This is very much like a plan Lee used at the Chickahominy, when he had Magruder make a demonstration south of the river, and sent D. H. Hill, A. P. Hill and Longstreet across at successive bridges, with Jackson closing the trap at the rear. We aren't sending the units in with quite the same pattern, but it's the same general idea. The advantage of our scheme is that Whaling goes in, and if he finds the going impossible, we haven't yet committed Hanneken and Puller, and we can revise our tactics.

"I think it'll work."

"All up! Let's go!"

The column started sluggishly up again. It wound up over the ridges, past a battery of 75's, through a gap in the double-apron barbed-wire barrier, and out into the beginnings of No Man's Land. After we came out on the last and highest ridge, Colonel Sims and I walked by a shortcut down to a coastwise road. We commandeered a jeep and rode forward as far as we could. This coast sector was where Colonel Edson, past master of the bush, was staging his holding attack. We asked our way to his command post.

Colonel Edson is not a fierce marine. In fact, he appears almost shy. Yet Colonel Edson is probably among the five finest combat commanders in all the American armed forces. "I hope the Japs will have some respect for American fighting men after this campaign," he says so quietly you have to lean forward to catch it all. "I certainly have learned respect for the Japs. What they have done is to take Indian warfare and apply it to the twentieth century. They use all the Indian tricks to demoralize their enemy. They're good, all right, but"— Colonel Edson's voice trails off to an embarrassed whisper—"I think we're better."

Edson's forward command post stood in the last of the palm trees, and consisted of a foxhole and a field telephone slung on a coconut tree. As we came up, he was sitting on the ground, hunched over, talking to one of his units on the phone.

When he was through phoning, Sims asked him what his situation was. "Only slight contact so far," he said. "We've met about a company of Japs on this side of the river, and they seem to be pretty well placed."

"I hope the muzzlers aren't pulling back," Sims said.

"Don't think so. They seem to have some mortars on the other side of the river, and I think they're pretty solid over there."

For the next two hours and more we were to witness some waiting which was nearly disastrous to the general plan. The waiting was caused by the watering of our force. The men had hiked more than ten miles under a broiling sun, and most had emptied their canteens. No one was certain when there would be another chance to water up—and water is the most precious commodity in human endurance. Therefore it was extremely important for the men to fill up.

The disaster was the way they filled up. The water source was a big trailer tank, which had been towed out from the camp by a truck. The tank had only one faucet, and each man had to file by, turn the faucet on, hold his canteen under it, and turn it off again. This took time, far too much time.

While the slow line moved by the tank, the men did not look like people about to be offered up for sacrifice; on the contrary, they looked like Americans waiting for a ball game to start, or merely getting rid of Saturday afternoon.

A lanky private named George E. Morgan sat on the hood of a jeep, reading an article by Walter Winchell, entitled *Americans We Can Do Without.* He looked up from his article, and said: "This Winchell sure is right: makes you sick to think about all the rackets that are going on at home while there's a war out here. Did you hear the scuttlebutt about Winchell being killed in an airplane accident?"

Across the road, Abner Partee ("Private, sir—most popular rank in the service") played his accustomed game of pretending to shirk. One of his officers told me he was actually a pretty hardworking fellow, but he certainly liked to talk, in his lazy Georgia drawl, about doing less.

"I got a hunderd thirty rounds of machine gun ammunition over here I'm a-hankerin' to fire. If I should happen to shoot a mess of Japs, and if I should happen to run out'n ammunition, then I reckon I wouldn't have to carry it, would I?"

The only intense scene I saw in the whole two hours of watering was a boy sitting beside the road against a tree trunk reading what must have been ten large pages of closely packed writing. The paper was crumpled and soiled: obviously he had read the letter right into his memory. After he finished, this time, he tore the pages in two, then tore the halves into quarters, and kept on tearing until there was a pathetic little confetti of farewell beside that Guadal road.

We turned off the beach road and cut up through a jungle defile parallel to the Matanikau. Now we were really moving into position, and word was passed that we must be on the lookout for snipers. The trail led us constantly upward. Occasionally we would break out onto a grassy knoll, then plunge back into the jungle.

By 3:15 our column had emerged on the crest of a broad and fairly high ridge which looked down over the whole area of battle. It was here that I first came to understand the expression "the fog of war." We thought we knew where we were, then found we didn't, then found it wasn't too easy to find out. All around us there was a maze of ridges like ours fringed with scallops of jungle. The Matanikau was hidden from our view by intervening ridges, so that we were not very sure of its course.

Fortunately we were high enough to see the coastline: we could figure out where we were by triangulation. One of the men took a bearing on Point Cruz, off to our left. Then he took a bearing on Lunga Point, back where the camp lay. He drew the two lines of bearing on the map, tangent to the tips of the points—and where the lines crossed was supposed to be our position. The first time we tried it, the lines crossed in jungle on the map, and we were on top of a ridge. The compass needle was wobbly, and it was necessary to take an average of the extremities of its wobbles. It was not the kind of compass work that would have pleased a sealubber. But the second try seemed a little more reasonable, and by sending a runner to investigate the configuration of a clump of trees, we were able to establish exactly where we were.

Lieutenant Colonel Puller's men were following us up the trail. When Colonel Sims found where we were, he told Colonel Puller that we would have to push on, even though darkness might shut down before we got to the prearranged bivouac. Now Colonel Puller is one of the hardest marine officers to restrain, once he gets started. He is as proud of his men as they are of him. And so when Colonel Sims told him to move on, he threw out his chest, blew out his cheeks, and said: "That's fine. Couldn't be better. My men are prepared to spend the night right on the trail. And that's the best place to be if you want to move anywhere."

Colonel Frisbie overheard this and couldn't resist giving The Puller a rib. "Gwan," he said, "we know your men are tough. The trouble with the trails along these ridges is that there's not enough horse dung for your men to use as pillows."

As we moved forward, the high flat snap of Jap snipers' rifles became more and more frequent. Once in a while, from nowhere, a lone bullet would sing over our heads, and hundreds of men would involuntarily duck, even though the bullet was long past. The worst seemed to come from a valley ahead and to the left of us. Down there Whaling was trying to force his way through to the river, and his men were meeting not only sniper fire but occasional machine-gun and mortar fire. When I looked at the faces of a handful of Colonel Sims's young men, who by now were already friends of mine—C. B., Bill, Ralph, Irving, Ted—I saw that they were no longer boastful joking lads. The music in that valley made them almost elderly.

Our bivouac for the night was on a ridge right above the valley, and we hardly had time to set up our radio equipment and to get the field telephone working when the walking wounded began to dribble up the awful incline out of the valley: young fellows with bandages wrapped scarf-like around their necks or with arms in slings, or with shirts off and a huge red and white patch on the chest. They struggled up that forty-five degree slope, absolutely silent about what they had seen and how they felt, most with a cigaret dangling lifelessly, perhaps unlit, out of one corner of the mouth, their eyes varnished over with pain.

Near the equator, the sun rises at about six and sets at about six all year round. By a quarter past six that night, it was nearly dark. An overcast was settling down: it looked like rain.

Gradually our bivouac settled down for the night. The men snuggled down into whatever comfortable spots they could find. They couldn't find many, because Guadal's ridges came up, once upon a time, out of the sea, and their composition is nine-tenths crumbled coral—not the stuff of beauty-rest.

C. B. had had the sense, as I had not, to look for a comfortable bed before it got pitch dark. The spot he picked was at the military crest: not on top of the ridge, but a little down the side—so that we would not be silhouetted at dawn, and so that sniper fire from the opposite side of the ridge could not reach us. Somehow he had found a place about twelve feet wide and six feet long where the coral was quite finely crumbled. When he heard me stumbling around and cursing coral, he called me over. I took off my pack and my canteen, folded my poncho double, and settled down. There was nothing to serve as pillow except either my pack, which was full of ration cans, or my steel helmet. I finally found that the most comfortable arrangement was to put my helmet on, and let it contend with the coral.

"Well, what do you think of the Marines?" C. B. asked.

I told him I was sold.

"They're a pretty fine bunch," he said. "Lots of this particular gang are pretty green, but they're willing and bright. There's no bitching among the privates in the Marine Corps for two reasons. The first is that they're all volunteers. If one of them starts talking back, the officer says: 'Nobody drafted you, Mac,' and every time, the squawker stops squawking. The other thing is that these men are a really high type. In peacetime the Corps only accepted about twenty percent of the applicants. In fact, the only difference between our officers and our privates is luck. One fellow got a break that the other didn't happen to get, and so he has the advantage of position."

C. B. started talking then about the enemy. "They're full of tricks," he said. "You'll see that when you go into the jungle after them. They hide up in the trees like wildcats. Sometimes when they attack, they scream like a bunch of terrified cattle in a slaughter house. Other times they come on so quiet they wouldn't scare a snake. One of their favorite tricks is to fire their machine guns off to one side. That starts you shooting. Then they start their main fire under the noise of your own shooting. Sometimes they use firecrackers as a diversion. Other times they jabber to cover the noise of their men cutting through the underbrush with machetes. You've probably heard about their using white surrender flags to suck us into traps. We're onto that one now. . . ."

And suddenly, like a child falling off in the middle of a bedtime story, C. B. was breathing hard and regularly. From then on, the night was in my hands, and I didn't like it.

My bedroom was the hollow empty sky, and every once in a while a 105-mm. shell would scream in one window and out the other. We lay within two hundred yards of where the shells were landing, and we heard the peculiar drilling sound you get only on the receiving end of artillery fire. All through the night snipers took pot shots at the ridges.

It was five in the morning before I dropped off. At five-thirty it started raining, and I woke up again. So did all the marines. The poncho helped, but rain infiltrates better than the Japs. Soon a spot here, a patch there, got wet. With the damp came chills, and before long there were a lot of miserable marines. The only consolation was that across the way there were undoubtedly a lot of miserable Japs.

The artillery and plane barrage that morning was a grim show from our grandstand ridge. The climax of the show was when two TBF's, the Navy's most graceful planes, came over and dropped two strings of hundred-pound bombs. From our ridge we could see the bombs leave their bays, describe their parabola, and fall, terribly, exactly where they were intended to fall. All along our ridge and the next, the marines stood up and cheered.

When the barrage subsided, huge white birds circled in terror over the jungle across the way and we had visions of the Japs circling in terror underneath. Bill, evidently thinking of them, said quietly: "War is nice but peace is nicer."

All that morning, while time seemed so important to a layman, we waited. The plan was for Whaling to force his crossing, after which Sims's men, under Hanneken and Puller, would follow through.

We settled down to wait for Whaling to have success. A few of us crept out on a knoll which towered above the river itself; we could

Jungle Warfare

Dogfight

Listening Post

Point

Lunga Bridge 8 Aug 42

Runner

Working Party

look down on the area where Whaling's men were doing their bitter work, and we could hear the chatter of their guns, but we could see no movement, so dense was the growth. In mid-morning we did see seven Japs running away up a burnt-off ridge across from us. A machine gun about twenty feet from us snapped at their heels, and they dived for cover. "How do you like the sound of that gun?" crowed one of the gunners. "That's the best damn gun in the regiment—in the Corps, for that matter."

At 11:40 A.M. the first of Whaling's men appeared on the ridges across the river. A signalman semaphored back the identification of the unit, so that we would not fire on them. At 11:45 A.M. Whaling sent a message back that the crossing had been secured. Colonel Hanneken's men began to move.

It was time for me to join a unit and go down.

Captain Charles Alfred Rigaud, standing there in the drizzle about to lead his heavy machine gun company into an impossible situation, looked like anything except a killer who took no prisoners. He had a boy's face. There were large, dark circles of weariness and worry under his eyes. His mustache was not quite convincing.

We stood on a high grassy ridge above a three hundred foot cliff, across from another, similar ridge. Between the two ridges lay the impossibility: a valley of unbelievably thick jungle. In the valley there was a little stream which ran into the Matanikau River.

I had walked along the ridge asking the men of the company who their commanding officer was.

They had said: "The Captain, along the line there."

It was not easy to find him, because all the officers had removed insignia from their uniforms: the shiny little bars might catch snipers' eyes. I walked up to two burly fellows, who had expressions of command on their unshaven faces, and asked if either of them was the captain.

"No," one of them said, "you want Captain Rigaud," and they pointed farther along.

When I finally came on him, he was talking quietly to a couple of his platoon leaders. I was surprised that such a slight, fragile body, with shoulders so stooped and such a soft voice, should be the commander.

I asked: "Are you the Captain?"

"I am Rigaud," he said.

"Where are you headed?"

"Down there." He pointed into the valley. "Our mission is to clear the valley of snipers, get to the river, and force a crossing."

"Is that a tough assignment?"

Captain Rigaud looked as if he thought it would be, but he said: "Whaling's outfit has already crossed the river farther up, and they're supposed to be working around behind the Japs opposite here. If we catch 'em between two fires, it ought to be easy.

Captain Rigaud had no way of knowing that Whaling's force was going to run into trouble as it tried to outflank the Japs—and that therefore Rigaud's mission in the valley was to be doomed before it got very far under way.

I asked if I could go along with him.

"You can go if you want to," he said, as if any one who would want to was crazy. My valor was certainly of ignorance; if I had had any understanding of what Company H might meet, I never would have gone along.

What happened to Company H in that valley happened in the particular way it did because of the particular kind of person Captain Rigaud was. In the valley I found out what the surface of him was like; since then I have learned a few details of what was underneath.

About nine and one half thousand miles to the northeast of the valley on Guadal, there is a house which is low, shingled with wood, and painted a very light color. It is on a small farm within the corporation of the village of Oriskany Falls, New York. Except for one, the rooms of this house are all on one floor, and they include a living room, dining room, kitchen and three bedrooms. One small bedroom is located upstairs. Rig's room was a good-sized bedroom in the right rear corner of the house. It was always very tidy when he was home, and his clothes were always hung up as neatly as possible because he always took the best care of them. In the morning his room was situated so as to fill right up with sunshine, like a glass with sweet cider.

There used to be music in the house. Rig began to play the violin when he was seven years old, taking lessons from a man named Frank Brock. At first it was often painful, when all he could produce was a whine from the open strings and his left arm got so tired from holding it as Mr. Brock said he must, so that he could see his elbow on the right side of the fiddle. But later, when he began to learn the second and third positions, and could play such things as *Salut d'Amour,* it was not bad. Later still, he carried his violin back and forth to school and played in the orchestra there, and then he went for lessons about twenty miles into Utica, at the Conservatory of Music.

His music began to be a pleasure. He used to play by the hour with his uncle, a piano player. One piece they used to play a great deal was *Joan of Arc,* by a composer whose name it is easy to forget. One of his sisters also used to play the piano with him, though not quite so well; and his younger brother Sidney took up the tuba, but that didn't go terribly well with the violin.

He liked both classical music and dance music. He played with the Oriskany Falls Church Civic Orchestra, but he also used to play very gaily at dances at the Falls and over at Franklin Springs. These were mostly square dances.

Rig liked dances very much. He liked girls very much, and they liked him. He never had any trouble getting dances. But he never did seem to get serious about any one girl, because he looked ahead and decided there was no place in his life for a woman, as yet. He was always as neat as possible around girls, his hair and clothes had to be just so. But he never talked seriously about marriage and such, because he wanted to do certain things in life first.

He was very ambitious. His father's father and his father were both barbers. They had had a shop together until Grandfather Rigaud grew too old for trimming with a razor. Rig's father was a very nice man who was perfectly devoted to his home and children, but Rig did not want to be a barber. He wanted to make some money and get out into the world.

He would work for a dollar wherever he could get it. He used to work as a gas station attendant for the uncle of his chum, Charles Engle, he mowed lawns around the town, and he would wash windows for Mr. Covell, the station master.

And he took his work in school quite seriously. When Rig went there, the high school was just a wooden structure, very small. There were two stories, the grades on the lower floor and the junior and senior high upstairs. On the roof there was a belfry which concealed a large bell which used to ring at school time. Rig was almost always on hand when the last bell rang. He was very studious and naturally intelligent above the average, and for all four years his marks were over ninety. He excelled especially in mathematics, for he got a hundred in elementary and intermediate algebra; he got ninety-eight in plane geometry. When it came to reading, he would always choose something historical, such as a book about Lafayette (he even preferred historical movies to any others). He would always argue with the teacher when he thought he was right, and one day, when the teacher and one of the girls in history class began talking about something entirely beside the point, Rig said right out: "All right, let's get back to history."

But he wasn't stuck in the mud. He always found time for a laugh in school, and he was always planning something. He called Charles Engle "Mac," and he would always be saying: Mac, let's go to the dance at Madison or let's go roller skating or let's go have a good old wiener roast, for he always had a suggestion.

And he was very playful with the girls and even the teachers. There was one teacher—she was tiny—who asked him one day to hand her a piece of chalk. Rig reached into the holder and grabbed two pieces, one short and one long. He started to hand her the long piece but suddenly changed his mind and gave her the short piece because she was so tiny, saying: "I'll give you the short one as you can't handle the other one."

His favorite sports were not of the usual kind, although he played an average game of basketball. What he liked best was to be outdoors.

Rig was right at home on a horse's back, and for several years he had a pure white pony named Queenie. After that he and Mac used to go over to a nearby farmer in Pleasant Valley who had riding horses, and they would never miss the horse races at Brookfield Fair. Brookfield is a small town tucked way back in the country, beautiful and mysterious

country, where the notorious Loomis gang once lived. The fairgrounds
were outside the village, and woods and hills were all around. The Fair
was the same as any city carnival, except that the grounds embraced a
race track a mile around. A small grandstand stood to one side of the
track, and between the stand and the track there was a platform where
vaudeville acts were put on. Then there were horse races, both riding
and trotting. The crowd would be made up entirely of people from
the surrounding rural communities, mostly farmers and their wives.
Rig and Mac would pick out horses they thought were going to win,
but they would never bet any money on their choices, for although
their choices were often very good, their money was not often very
plentiful.

The two friends used to go hunting together. They used to put a
coin against a tree and shoot at it, and Rig proved to be a crack shot.
He loved to go after pheasant, which he would do with the help of
an English setter, Bessie, who adored him. In late years when he came
home from college, Bessie would bound all over the large yard around
the house and then around the barn and through the vegetable garden
and into the pasture and back, crazy-happy. With Bessie, Rig and Mac
would go out and bag some pheasant or rabbit or grey squirrel.

They also trapped. One fall they went around to look at their traps
and they had a skunk in one. He was very much alive, and they were
trying to figure out how to kill him without getting plastered when Rig
suddenly lifted his hatchet and threw it at him. The butt end hit the
skunk in the head and the problem was over. He was a quarter-stripe
skunk, and the pair hung him up on a clothes line and picked the white
fur out of him so as to get more money. The fur buyer never noticed
and the boys got the price of a black skunk.

There was nothing Rig liked better than to cook and eat what they
shot. In the still of a crisp autumn evening, they would go over to Lake
Morraine, a small lake about two miles long. Midway on the lake was
a piece of land which stuck out into the water. They called this The
Point. Out there on The Point they would build an open fire and roast
their game and eat it with exclamations of self-satisfaction. Opposite
The Point there was a dancehall where they used to dance quite often,
and although Rig was an excellent dancer and fond of it, whenever he

was on The Point he would say how glad he was not to be over there in the dance hall.

Besides all the play, though, there was quite a bit of work around home. His father kept four or five cows, and they had to be filled up and drained all the time. And there were things to do in the house, helping his mother. Fortunately there were the others—Ralph and Sidney and Helen and Phyllis—to lend their hands, too.

Rig's mother was a good mother. Of medium height, slender, with cheeks rosier than rouge and a very sweet smile, she was always at home, entirely absorbed in the rearing of her children. She was always confident that her children would do the right thing, and as they grew older she left them very much on their own. She was always generous, and if anything alarmed her, she hid what she felt. She was a good mother.

It had been Rig's ambition to go to West Point. "He had the brains," they say at the Falls, "but not the drag, that is the trouble with our country today, they don't pick a man on his merits, it's just who he knows." And so when the West Point thing fell through, he picked the Forestry College at Syracuse. At Syracuse he worked very hard, especially on his R.O.T.C. course. Mac went up to help him graduate, and he watched Rig proudly and enviously as he got his diploma. Senator Vandenberg gave the address. Rig graduated as a second lieutenant in the U. S. Army.

But he had his heart set on the Marines. He went down to New York to take his physicals, passed them, and went off to Philadelphia for basic training. He graduated as a second lieutenant of Marines in the month when the Nazis broke through into the Lowlands.

Everybody in Oriskany Falls thought that the Marines were very good for Rig, and his close friends knew that he was good for the Marines. When he came home, he looked so spruce and neat and confident.

Of course it was very hard when he had to go away for good. A lot of people missed him around the town; girls as well as boys. But most of all, of course, his mother missed him. She continued to be very brave, for she could see the constant danger of his life, and yet she would not show her concern. She worried constantly but she would tell Mac that

Rig was doing exactly as he wanted to do and nothing could change his ideas.

He was really something to be proud of, after all. "Well," he wrote in one of his letters, "as you probably have suspected I am a true veteran now. I have been through Tulagi and Guadalcanal which no doubt you have read about. And we really slapped the Japs. That's about all I can tell you of the operation."

And later: "I am alive and well and after what I've seen that is the most you can ask for. Don't worry about me, I am having fun and getting campaign ribbons. I was recommended for decoration on Tulagi."

Apparently life was not too serious. "It is very hot and real tropical here," he wrote. "The Hotel Coral Gables is my lean-to made of palm leaves. Somebody tacked that sign on it."

And he seemed to be with fine men. He wrote: "I still have my same command, and believe me they are a fighting outfit—not a boy in the lot, although some are very young—I must be getting old."

But the thing that was nicest was when he talked about home. Sometimes he did it jokingly, like this: "Some men got magazines in the mail. We laugh at a lot of this U.S.O. stuff for the Army, etc. I guess they forget all about the Marines but we'll do the fighting."

But sometimes he was serious, as when he wrote:

"I'd like to be home now. The Fall is so nice."

Captain Rigaud's company was a veteran unit. His boys were blooded. They had been in every battle so far, and with the possible exception of Edson's Raiders, a gang of bush-fighting specialists, there was no unit which had been in such tough spots. They had learned that war is a hard bargainer: for a handful of minor successes they had had to pay dearly—twenty-two young, unfulfilled lives.

They were proud of their toughness, and while Captain Rigaud went up and down the line giving quiet orders for the descent, two non-coms took me in hand to make sure that I understood their worth.

"You should've seen where they put us that awful night on Lunga Ridge when the Japs almost got through to the airfield," one said.

The other said: "They always give us the dirty work."

"We was at the Tenaru River, too," the first said. "That was where we really laid 'em out in stacks."

"They always send us in for the mean jobs," said the second.

"We got the best damn machine gun platoons in the regiment. And I guess mortar batteries don't come any better than our battery. Old Lou Diamond runs it—ever heard of him? Too bad his bunch isn't around so you could see for yourself."

"Yeah," said the second, "look where they've got old Lou now: down by the beach with the holding attack: heaviest work of the whole damn battle."

Most marines boast about their unit, but it happens that I had seen Lou Diamond's battery in action and had been told by impartial men that it was one of the best batteries in the whole Corps. If the rest of Rigaud's men were as good, I was in steady hands. The reason I had found out about Lou Diamond was that while visiting Colonel Edson's command post in the area of the holding attack the day before, I had heard a mortar battery making twice the racket a mortar battery usually makes. The extra noise was shouting. When I asked whose it was, I was told that the voice belonged to Master Gunner Sergeant Lou Diamond, who was said to be approximately two hundred years old.

Presently I saw him—a giant with a full grey beard, an admirable paunch, and the bearing of a man daring you to insult him. They told me that Lou was so old that there was some question whether to take him along on such a hazardous job as the Solomons campaign. He was getting too unwieldly to clamber up and down cargo nets. On one of the last days before embarkation, Lou found that they were debating about his antiquity. So he went out and directed loading operations with such violence that for a time he lost his voice entirely; the next morning he was told he could go along.

Here he was, proving that even if he out-Methuselahed Methuselah, he would still be the best damn mortar man in the Marines. As we went by, he was, as usual, out of patience. He wanted to keep on firing, and had been told to hold back. "Wait and wait and wait and wait," he roared. "God, some people around here'll fall on their ass from waiting. . . ."

And so hearing that Lou Diamond was in Rigaud's company

clinched my trust in it. But even without Diamond, these men looked like the sort you would pick for bodyguard on a dark night. This was especially true if you looked, not at their faces, but at their gear and physique.

The only element of uniformity was their battle dress. "Utilities," as they are called, are of tough green cloth, which will neither tear nor show in the jungle. The shirt has an open collar, loose sleeves, and, over the heart, a patch pocket with the Marine Corps insignia, a globe symbolizing the Marines' ubiquitousness (they are proud of it: *"From the halls of Montezuma to the shores of Tripoli . . ."*). The pants are generous, like overalls. Most of Company H had their pants tucked into their socks, or tied snug around their ankles; many had them tied, as I did, with pieces of captured Japanese straw rope.

But aside from their utilities, they were as various and vicious looking as a bunch of pirates. No two packs were of the same size. Each man brought just what he thought he would want and need. The minimum was a poncho, a canteen, rations and a spoon. More provident men had slipped in a few symbols, at least, of comfort: cigarets in little watertight tins, salt tablets to compensate for sweat, small first aid packages.

Every man had sneaked along something he thought no one else had—something he had wheedled from the quartermaster or swiped from a store-tent. Before our departure from camp a young captain had taken me into his tent and slipped me two extra bars of Ration D, the chocolate ration, which he said he had gotten never mind where. "In the Marines it's every man for himself as far as equipment goes," he said.

Captain Rigaud's men were certainly armed in this spirit. Each man was weaponed to his own taste and heart's content. Captain Rigaud himself carried one of the handiest of Marine weapons, a Browning automatic rifle. The company's proper weapons, heavy machine guns, were carried dismantled, one man carrying the barrel assembly, another the tripod, and a whole squad the ammunition, in heavy metal boxes. But even some of the men assigned to machine guns carried personal arms. Some of the company had old 1903 bolt-action Springfields. Almost all carried knives, slung from their belts, fastened to their packs, or strapped to their legs. Several had field shovels, which they knew how to swing nastily. Some carried .45-calibre automatic pistols. Pockets bulged with grenades. Some were not satisfied with one bayonet, but carried two. There were even a couple of Japanese bayonets. The greatest refinement was an ugly weapon I spotted in the tunic pocket of a corporal—a twelve-inch screwdriver.

I asked him how he happened to bring that along.

"Oh," he said, "just found it on my person.

"When do you expect to use it?"

"Never can tell, might lose my bayonet with some Japs in the neighborhood."

But the faces of Captain Rigaud's men were not the faces of bullies. When you looked into the eyes of those boys, you did not feel sorry for the Japs: you felt sorry for the boys. The uniforms, the bravado, the air of wearing a knife in the teeth—these were just camouflage. The truth was all over those faces.

These were just American boys. They did not want that valley or any part of its jungle. They were ex-grocery clerks, ex-highway laborers, ex-bank clerks, ex-schoolboys, boys with a clean record and maybe a little extra restlessness, but not killers. They had volunteered; they had come into the Marines with their eyes open. Yes, but they had joined the Marines to see the world, or to get away from a guilt, or most likely to escape the draft, not knowingly to kill or be killed.

It would be unfair to say that there was fear on any single one of those faces. But neither was there elation. There certainly was weariness. In the last war men were almost never in front lines more than two weeks, but these boys had arrived on August seventh, and this day was October eighth, and every inch of the Guadal beachhead had been front line all along. On top of that they had slept one night in the field, tossing restlessly on stones and their anxiety. There was also hunger visible there. In two days they had eaten, at most, two units of Ration C and two of D—thirty ounces of meat and vegetable hash or stew, straight from the can, cold; eight ounces (equal to 600 calories) of chocolate, sugar, skim milk powder, cocoa fat, oat flour, vanillin, and 500 units of *thiamin hydrochloride* (vitamin B_1), sweet but dry as peanut butter.

But the truth on those faces was not just a physical thing. It was some shadow out of the mind, an uneasiness. It was a positive sign that if some lieutenant colonel had come up and given them their choice between going into that valley or going home, they would have said the hell with the valley.

That is what Company H was like, ready for action.

"The first platoon will go first. Third platoon follow. Headquarters next. Second platoon in the rear."

Captain Rigaud spoke his orders quietly, as if commenting on the weather. The company was scattered out along about two hundred yards of trail, and when the orders were passed, they rearranged themselves without hurry or excitement.

It surprised me to learn that we were going to advance in single file, as I had always pictured troops sneaking through the jungle in parallel waves. Later, when we got down into the valley, it was easy to see why we marched in Indian file. In order not to spend all day moving a hundred yards in that tangle, it was essential to stick to the trail. The trail was very narrow, and most of the time it had the stream on one side and a sudden upward steep on the other.

When the line was formed, Captain Rigaud moved up and down, not saying much, just looking his men over. When he reached the head of the line, one of the platoon leaders asked: "Where do you want us to start down?"

"What's the matter with right here?" Captain Rigaud pointed over the edge.

Three or four men moved forward, craned, and came back.

"Awful steep, Captain," one said.

"The ammunition's awful heavy," another said.

"No use to break our necks getting to the Japs, Captain," the platoon leader said. "Don't you think we better go around there, where we can go down a little easier?" He pointed to a bend in the ridge which was actually farther from the enemy than where we were then.

"Okay," Captain Rigaud said, "But let's get going."

He took his place with the headquarters group, and I fell in right behind him. The line started up slowly, walking at the apparently careless pace of men carrying heavy burdens. Our path wound along the military crest—just a few feet over the side from the top of the ridge.

I was glad that the path climbed to the top of the ridge at a spot where the ridge itself took a little rise: it gave me one last chance to see the view before going down into the valley. It was like a last deep breath of good air before diving into a dark, stagnant pool.

The drizzle gave the view a mysterious softness. The sea, which in the sunlight had looked as brittle as a blue plate, was now just a great vapor. Florida and Tulagi, across the channel, seemed merely immobilized low-lying smoke. To the northwest on Guadal, Cape Esperance melted into the overcast above it. Nearer, jungle fought with bare ridges all along the curve of the bay. Point Cruz, a tiny, Florida-shaped peninsula covered with thickest jungle, reached out into the sea just beyond a depressed and steamy tangle which we knew to be our objective, the Matanikau. Behind us, where the camp lay, we could see the regular swatches of Lever Bros. coconut palms, whose fruit of that season was not destined for bars of soap.

In the drizzle the contrast between the high, grassy ridges and the jungle valleys was more noticeable than ever. The low clouds made the day seem closed in, and only on the open heights was there any freedom: the jungle below looked especially dark and confined. On the way up to the front, we had come through patches of jungle, and it had seemed alien, almost poisonous. The vegetation closed in tightly on either side of the trail, a tangle of nameless trees and vines. It was lush without being beautiful; there were no flowers, and the smell of the place was dank rather than sweet. Each time we came out into the light on the grassy knolls, we breathed deeply and more easily. These open spaces were our natural terrain. They were American; the jungle was Jap.

I found that these reactions were not just mine. All through the battle, the Americans tended to stick to the grassy heights, the Japs to the jungle valleys. Of course, each had to explore the others' domain. The marines had to descend into the snarl and clean out the Japs, as we were about to do; and the Japs, when they wanted to strike back, had to charge the hills. Each side derived certain advantages from following its bent. On the ridges, the Americans could dominate the jungle with their fire-power, and they could see what was going on. In the jungle, the Japs could hide themselves in ambush, and they could lead the Americans into easy traps.

Now as we went over the edge of the ridge, leaving the soft day to go into the distasteful place below, I couldn't help wondering what Rigaud's men were thinking about. I was miserably green, and had no idea what to expect. This was fortunate, for it kept me from being afraid. Mostly I was curious, inquisitive. I was almost elated over the prospect of being baptized in fire; I felt that I was going to have a great experience. But Company H had had this experience. They were veterans, and would have no use for such thoughts.

Probably many of them were afraid, since they had the necessary knowledge. Many of them probably had brief thoughts, as I did, of home. But what I really wondered was whether any of them gave a single thought to what the hell this was all about. Did these men, who might be about to die, have any war aims? What were they fighting for, anyway?

Not only down the first slippery steep, but far along the trail into the jungle I wondered about this, until I asked, and got a strange answer, as you will see.

By the time this heavily loaded company had tramped and slid and stumbled in the rain down the grassy pass into the valley, there was nothing left of the forty-five degree slope but a muddy slick, in which there could be no such thing as a foothold. Toward the end of the column, several men crashed to the ground and skidded with their burdens as much as twenty feet.

The jungle was narrow at the point where we entered, and fairly thin. The little stream, which we were going to cross and recross, cut through this thin place with quick little rapids, as if it were impatient with the sparseness and wanted to get back into really snug jungle.

Most of us were terribly thirsty. Green men like myself had failed to conserve the water in our canteens, and many had gone without a drink overnight. And so many of us waded a few feet upstream and filled up.

As I bent over and put my canteen under water a marine next to me, who was filling his, whispered: "Can't tell who's dead upstream."

One of Captain Rigaud's platoon leaders, a tall, slender Ohio boy named Lieutenant Donald Peppard, dropped four drops of iodine in my canteen from his pocket first aid kit; I shook it up, waited a few minutes, and drank. The water was brown, pharmaceutical-smelling, and had a definite upstream taste; but it sure was good.

About a hundred yards further on, after we had forded the stream a second time, the jungle suddenly became stiflingly thick. This was enemy territory in earnest.

Our column moved in absolute silence. It is impossible to describe the creepy sensation of walking through that empty-looking but crowded-seeming jungle.

What made it eerie was that the jungle was far from silent. The birds whose cries had sounded so cheerful from the heights were terrifying now. Parakeets and macaws screeched from nowhere. There was one bird with an altogether unmusical call which sounded exactly like a man whistling shrilly through his fingers three times—and then another, far off in Japanese territory, would answer. The stream made a constant noise, and an annoying one. It seemed terribly important to listen for the enemy (as if the Japs would be so stupid as to crackle through the underbrush), but the stream's continuous chatter, maddeningly cheerful, made that impossible in any case. Off and on we could hear the noises of our own power—planes and artillery—far above the jungle roof. These should have been encouraging noises: up on the ridges they had been. But down here the noises were merely weird—the eccentric whirr of the strafing P-39s, sounding as if some big cog in each engine were unlubricated; the soft, fluttery sound of shells in flight, like the noise a man would make if he were to blow through a keyhole.

Tiny noises became exaggerated in our minds. Drops of accumulated drizzle would crash down onto fallen leaves like heavy footfalls. The click of a canteen cover belonging to one of our own men at some point where the trail doubled back beyond a screen of jungle sounded like a whole machine gun being set up. And then when some really big noise would break out—a dead tree falling over at this of all times—our whole column would jump with caricatured vigilance.

Captain Rigaud leaned forward and whispered to the man in front of him, who leaned forward in turn and whispered to the next man.

Then Captain Rigaud turned to me and whispered: "Pass the word to keep five paces."

I didn't quite understand what he meant and said so.

Patiently he whispered: "I want the men to keep five paces apart, so as not to get all bunched up and give snipers big targets."

And so the message hissed forward and backward along the line in a whisper:

"Keep five paces."

"Keep five paces."

"Keep five paces. . . ."

In news accounts of the fighting on Bataan I had read about the ingenious ways in which Jap snipers hid themselves in the trees: dressed all in green, hands and face painted green, foliage caught in headnets and slung from the waist—all made to look exactly like parts of the trees into which they were tied once and for all. All along the way I saw bunches up in the trees and could only hope they were not human; there was absolutely no way of telling. During one halt I noticed a hollow in one huge tree trunk, and in the hollow what seemed to be the head and left shoulder of a man, and below that a small point which I imagined to be a muzzle. In trying to make sure, I showed myself, and drew no fire. I'm still not sure, in the light of what happened later, that that shape was not a Japanese shape.

Now I comprehended for the first time why the marines had been taking so few prisoners. It was not just that the boys were trigger-happy, as one had boasted. It was not just brutality, not just vindictive remembrance of Pearl Harbor. Here in the jungle a marine killed because he must, or be killed. He stalked the enemy, and the enemy stalked him, as if each were a hunter tracking a bear cat.

I remembered what a marine had said to me back in the comfort of the camp: "I wish we were fighting against Germans. They are human beings, like us. Fighting against them must be like an athletic performance—matching your skill against someone you know is good. Germans are misled, but at least they react like men. But the Japs are like animals. Against them you have to learn a whole new set of physical reactions. You have to get used to their animal stubbornness and tenacity. They take to the jungle as if they had been bred there, and like some beasts you never see them until they are dead."

When we had entered the first, thick stretch of jungle, I could have imagined no greater tenseness. But as we sneaked forward, the feeling of tightness steadily increased. When the next word was passed along the line, there was a little climax of tenseness. This message came back from the head of the column and must have been originated by the platoon leader there.

The word came slowly, in whispers, for it was a long message:

"Keep sharp lookout to right and to left."

"Keep sharp lookout to right and to left."

"Keep sharp lookout to right and to left. . . ."

As if we had to be told! After this word, another kind of message came back along the line: the tiny clicks of bullets being slipped into the chambers of weapons.

Unfortunately for my sense of security, there is a thing called the Geneva Convention, which the United States humanely (and out of fear of reprisal) still observes. Under it, correspondents are noncombatants, and travel armed at their own risk. I would have felt more comfortable in that valley near the breach of some 155-mm. howitzer, I think. As it was, the nearest weapon of any consequence was Captain Rigaud's Browning, which he held over his left arm, ready for instant use.

It was probably because I was a bad soldier, and looked at the ground rather than up in the trees, that I stumbled on my first really tangible evidence of the enemy.

We were moving very slowly now. It seemed strange to me to be walking erect. I had imagined men in the jungle slithering along on their bellies, or at least creeping on all fours, like animals; but we didn't even stoop.

Each man studied each tree. The Marines, looking up, walked with sure feet, as if some extra sense told them where each hummock and tricky root lay in the trail. After a couple of stumbles which were as humiliating as they were noisy, I learned to watch my step.

While watching it, at a point where a huge tree trunk pressed close against the trail, I saw what appeared to be a bunched piece of green cloth, about the size of a handkerchief, lying on the ground. I picked it up and found it was a sniper's headnet.

It was made of light green cord, and looked like a small minnow net. Leaves and little branches had evidently been stuck in the holes, for some of the strings were torn.

I touched Captain Rigaud on the arm, and held the net out for him to see. Without changing the look of his face, he merely nodded and shaped one soundless word with his lips: "Jap."

Belatedly it occurred to me to look up in the tree. No one was there. The owner of the headnet had evidently taken himself off in a hurry. We wondered if he had heard us and been intimidated by our numbers; or perhaps he had gone back to warn his companions.

This thing in my hand, this symbol of the animal wiles our men find so hard to understand, brought me for the first time face to face with the enemy as an individual, not just as an idea. I had long hated the idea but I did not hate this individual: he had never done me any harm (though he might at any moment, I realized somewhat too vividly). I wondered where he was from—perhaps from some steep village in the mountains of Hakone, perhaps from a quiet place by the inland sea, perhaps from up north in Hokkaido, where the men are tall and rugged. Conscription had snatched him from his hopes, and young friends had sat at a banquet table and brushed arrogant characters on the little flag he was to carry to the front. He had taken some hard lessons in killing, probably in Shantung or Hainan or Luzon. He had packed a little cooked rice, and a little uncooked, into his knapsack, and then with the Emperor's praises ringing in his skull, he had come forward, and strapping his pole-climber's jacks to his ankles, had climbed into this tree, pulled this headnet over his worried head, and settled down to wait, invisible.

Then, for some reason and at some moment just before our arrival, he had scrambled down out of the tree and run. I had heard that Japanese soldiers never had the imagination to run away. For a Japanese, this individual was a pleasant surprise. I put his headnet over my own helmet.

Having seen this first token of the enemy, being sure now that the enemy was a reality, I was much more serious about scanning the trees on either side of the trail. Before finding the net, I had thought Captain Rigaud's vigilance just a little exaggerated, like something out of an unconvincing movie. But now he seemed exactly natural: my own neck started from its socket at just as tight an angle as his.

By now the trail was really rough. There would be sudden rises and sheer drops of ten feet, and sometimes the gully of the stream would interrupt it sharply. The stream crossings for the most part came where little spines of coral cut across the gully, forming little dams. The column picked its way carefully across these dams—carefully because a misstep would mean a ducking and too much noise. The stream was beginning to widen here, for it was almost ready to marry the Matanikau.

At one point the trail ran fairly level, close alongside the right bank of the stream, with just a narrow screen of bamboos and occasional big trunks separating us from it. At one opening I happened to look at the water and jumped when I saw, half under water and half out, weirdly pointing right at me, a rifle.

It had a very short stock and a very long barrel—not like any American type I had seen. Again I touched Captain Rigaud's arm and when he looked around I pointed. He nodded again, and without changing his expression shaped the same word: "Jap."

How this rifle had gotten in the middle of the stream all by itself had just begun to puzzle me when suddenly, up ahead, three or four rifle shots—the high-pitched, Jap kind—broke the silence.

Almost at once a message came cantering back along the line:

"Hold it up."

"Hold it up."

"Hold it up. . . ."

Snipers had apparently found a target to their liking. Our column would have to wait while those up at the head, doubtless under cover now, tried to find the enemy sharpshooter.

As we waited I wondered if any of those Japanese bullets had found a mark, and I thought back to something I had been told about dead marines the night before we set out from camp.

A Lieutenant Colonel and I had been sitting on canvas camp stools in front of the regimental commander's tent. The Lieutenant Colonel's name did not have a particularly marine sound about it: Julian Frisbie—but in the daylight he certainly looked and talked the part. He was about six feet two and must have weighed a muscular two hundred. He roared his commands and cursed the most miniature lagging. He was executive officer to Col. Amor Sims, the regimental commander, who later told me: "Julian and I can't run around doing the same things, so we have a deal: I'm to keep my mouth shut and he's to do all the shouting." Col. Frisbie was a fine shouter; his men called him The Bull Moose.

From supper until about eight o'clock that night he had been completely in character, telling me pungent stories of the toughness of marines. He was well up on his Marine Corps traditions and he often referred back to historical ruggednesses. But at about eight we were interrupted, and his mood suddenly changed.

A young officer of the watch hurried by us into the tent to wake Col. Sims and report that flares had been seen out to sea. We heard Col. Sims answer in his calm way that since his unit didn't know what they were, and since it had no facilities for finding out, there was no use worrying about them—just pretend they were lightning.

When the officer of the watch left for his post, Col. Frisbie no longer talked in a loud voice of fearlessness and skill. He said very quietly:

"Have you ever seen men killed on the field of battle?"

"No, the only dead people I've ever seen were drowned."

"Well," he said, "you'll probably see some out on this push. We've seen plenty since we've been on Guadal. Down at the Tenaru River, after our great battle there, there were nearly seven hundred dead Japs lying around. That wasn't too terrible. It's possible to think of dead enemy as dead animals. But there were a lot of our boys lying there too and that wasn't so good. You will see some of them in the next couple of days, I'm afraid. It's a pathetic sight. You'll see. They look just like dirty-faced little boys who have gone to bed without being tucked in by their mothers. . . ."

Here in the valley I was to get a vivid reminder of Colonel Frisbie's words. The line began to move again without any more shots having been fired. This meant, we in the middle of the line knew, that the sniper or snipers had not been found. There just wasn't time. We had quite a job to get done before dark; we would just have to take our chances on the rest of the line rooting this sharpshooter out.

Now for the first time I moved with a well-defined sense of hazard. The others, who knew more, had probably felt it all along. The sensation here was an acute version of one I had felt at sea, when a task force in which I was travelling went through waters infested with Japanese submarines, which occasionally fired torpedoes at us. The bad thing was that you never knew from which quarter you might be struck, or when. You were on the receiving end, and you could not see the thing about to strike you.

A few feet farther along I got the shock for which I thought I had braced myself. The trail rose suddenly; we helped ourselves up by pulling on the roots of trees higher up. Then the trail leveled off and took a short turn. And just beyond the turn lay a dead marine.

Captain Rigaud glanced back at me this time without my touching his arm. His lips did not shape any word, but his bitter, young face said, as plainly as if he had shouted it: "The Japs are bastards."

Somebody had straightened the dead boy out and closed his eyes and thrown a poncho over him. His face, though, was not entirely covered, and we couldn't help seeing it.

Colonel Frisbie was a tough old campaigner. He knew about these things. He was right.

A runner came hurrying back along the trail to Captain Rigaud. These runners are an anachronism. They make up human lines of communication; they do the jobs that copper wire and short waves ought to do, and they are expected by some commanding officers to do them as fast. They carry messages alone, often through enemy territory. Their fellows take them for granted, but there are no men who are braver or stronger.

This one reported to Captain Rigaud in a wind-swept whisper: "Sir, our scouts to right and forward have made contact with scouts of

George Company and Easy Company." (For phonetic convenience, English-speaking signalmen everywhere give letters the same names, in a sort of reverse primer. George is for G, Easy is for E, and we were Hypo Company.)

Captain Rigaud passed word both ways to hold the line up. Then he said to the runner: "Where in hell did they come from?"

The runner looked like a fellow who hasn't studied his lesson very well, then said: "Don't know, sir. I was just told to tell you what I told you already."

The platoon leaders converged on headquarters to see what was doing. One of them suggested that probably George and Easy had been detailed to work up the right bank of the Matanikau as far as this stream.

Then probably, another suggested, their left flank was supposed to touch our right flank when we got to the river, and we would then have a continuous front.

Probably, a third suggested, they were going to help us force a crossing of the river.

These probabilities all eventually proved to be truths but they were not enough to risk a company on, so Captain Rigaud sent the runner off to find out for sure.

Being caught in such uncertainty was no fun. This was not just being confused, as we had been the previous day. It was having slipped out of relationship to the whole operation. It was bumping into George and Easy and not knowing why. Worse, it was a sense of not having been told enough—just getting orders to clean out a valley and force a river and not knowing what the others were doing or what it all added up to.

And so after the brief whispered parley with the runner by the stream, I learned what it is like for men fighting a skirmish to feel that they have been sent out alone, that they, a small band, are fighting the whole damn show.

When caught this way by doubt, there is nothing to do except what the old sailing men down in Maine do when it blows in thick-o'-fog and you can't see from one island to the other: just wait it out. We in the valley waited for the runner to get back and clear things up.

War, as old Lou Diamond would certainly agree, seems to be nine-tenths waiting—waiting in line for chow, waiting for promotion, waiting for mail, for an air raid, for dawn, for reinforcements, for orders, for the men in front to move, for relief, for that runner.

At first, as we waited, we were tense. Captain Rigaud said as loudly as he could in a whisper: "All right there. Don't stand around now. Keep your eyes peeled."

But after a few minutes we got used to the place and we began to relax. Soon the Captain, his platoon leaders and I got into one of the strangest conversations I had ever heard. Even if everything that was said had been commonplace, it would have been strange, because it was all in whispers.

The men stood in a tight little knot right in the trail, where they had discussed the runner's news. Besides the Captain and myself, there were three platoon leaders: Lt. Donald Peppard, the tall one who had dropped iodine into my canteen; Lt. Gordon Calder, a Yale man, son of the President of American & Foreign Power Co.; and Lt. Robert Brizard, a stocky Ohioan. Except for Captain Rigaud's gambit, I shall not say which man said which things. Although the conversation might have taken place on any of several fronts, and any military men, from colonel to messboy, might have been the speakers, it would not be fair to identify specific men with specific words.

Captain Rigaud started it, by whispering to me, in comment on the confusion: "It's the same as always. They never tell us enough."

"Not only about what we're doing," another said. "We never get anything but the damndest scuttlebutt about what's going on in the world. We don't even know who's winning."

"Yeah," said a third. "Tell us what's going on." I was their most recent connection with the outside world, and they started pouring out questions.

"Are the Russians holding on?"

I said they had done much better than anyone had thought possible.

"Why the hell isn't Dugout Dug doing anything?"

I said that MacArthur had not been sent any supplies, except for the merest replacements, and no general could do anything with nothing—as he himself had said.

"Well why haven't they sent him anything?"

By this time I realized that they didn't really want answers to their questions. They just wanted to throw out their questions, as if they were merely waving their arms in angry gestures of protest.

"Are we going to be left holding the bag here, like those poor suckers in the Philippines?"

"Why the bejeezus hasn't the Navy had some PT boats in here sooner to stop that godawful shelling at night?"

"They always told us that marines were supposed to take some place, and then the Army would come along right away so as the marines could take something else. Where the hell's all the Army? They say some's coming in, but we're going to maybe stay. What's the use of that?"

"Can't they do something about the divided command out here? You'd think we were two allies, instead of the most powerful single nation on earth."

"Where's all that power, anyhow? Where's that world-beating P-47 we've heard so much about? Where's that famous new Navy fighter, what is it, the F4U? Where's all that great production?"

The questions became formulas:

" . . . strikes . . . ?"

" . . . politics . . . ?"

" . . . propaganda . . . ?"

This was my chance. Now was the time to ask these men what they were fighting for.

These men were not especial malcontents. I had heard questions like these asked by too many men to think this an outstanding group of complainants. But here they were, perhaps about to give their lives for their country, and yet exercising, until it nearly collapsed from being exercised, the right of free speech. How could men harboring such doubts and such protests fight with enthusiasm? What was there in it for them?

And so I said: "I wonder if I could ask you fellows one question. It's something I've been wondering about quite a bit here on this island. What would you say you were fighting for? Today, here in this valley, what are you fighting for?"

The excited flush, which had come into their faces as they asked their questions, went out again. Their faces became pale. Their eyes wandered. They looked like men bothered by a memory. They did not answer for what seemed a very long time.

Then one of them spoke, but not to me. He spoke to the others, and for a second I thought he was changing the subject or making fun of me, but of course he was not. He was answering my question very specifically.

He whispered: "Jesus, what I'd give for a piece of blueberry pie."

Another whispered: "Personally I prefer mince."

A third whispered: "Make mine apple with a few raisins in it and lots of cinnamon: you know, Southern style."

Fighting for pie. Of course that is not exactly what they meant. Here, in a place where they had lived for several weeks mostly on captured Japanese rice, then finally had gone on to such delicacies as canned corned beef and Navy beans, where they were usually hungry and never given a treat—here pie was their symbol of home.

In other places there are other symbols. For some men, in places where there is plenty of good food but no liquor, it is a good bottle of scotch whiskey. In other places, where there's drink but no dames, they say they'd give their left arm for a blonde. For certain men, books are the thing; for others, music; for others, movies. But for all of them, these things are just badges of home. When they say they are fighting for these things, they mean that they are fighting for home—"to get the goddam thing over and get home."

Perhaps this sounds selfish. It certainly sounds less dynamic than the Axis slogans. But home seems to most marines a pretty good thing to be fighting for. Home is where the good things are—the generosity, the good pay, the comforts, the democracy, the pie.

When the runner returned, he reported just what Rigaud's lieutenants had guessed—that George and Easy Companies had moved up to make contact with our right, and that they were to try to help force the river. He also reported that we were only about a hundred yards from the river.

Captain Rigaud passed this whispered order: "Advance and watch out for friendly troops on the right."

The men who were carrying machine gun parts seemed to bunch up together as we moved forward this time. They wanted to be ready to assemble their guns on shortest notice.

Occasional whispering, which had been visible though not audible along the line when we moved before, now stopped.

Men picked their footsteps carefully now.

Captain Rigaud's small back and stooped shoulders hardly moved up and down at all. His knees were a little bent, like those of a cat about to leap.

We crossed and recrossed the stream very carefully but rather hurriedly: no one wanted to be caught in the water. It was much wider now, much browner and more sluggish. We were apparently quite near the Matanikau.

Up ahead, as a matter of fact, some of Rigaud's men and a few of the men of George and Easy Companies had already crossed the river. No shots had been fired. There seemed to be no opposition: there was reason to hope that Whaling had already swept around behind whatever was on the other side and cleaned it out (we had heard some firing from the other side during the morning), so that now our job would be a pushover. Maybe, if we were lucky, just a sniper or two to hunt down and kill.

The trail left the stream, turned off to the right, and climbed up onto a spur. Up there, on the spur, we could see the thinning of the trees which meant the Matanikau. In a moment we would be at the river and, if Whaling had been as successful as we hoped, across it.

The captain and I were about seventy-five feet from the river when we found out how wrong our hope was.

The signal was a single shot from a sniper.

It came from somewhere behind us, but probably not as far as the first shots we had heard. The high flat snap was easily recognizable as a Japanese sound, and immediately after it, overhead, went the sound of the bullet, like a supercharged bee.

After a couple of too quick seconds, snipers all around us opened up. There would be the snap, and the whine, and then the tuck when the bullet went into the ground. There was no way of knowing where the next was coming from. The only thing you could be certain of was that it would come soon enough to take your eye off the place where you thought you might spot the last one.

Then machine guns from across the river opened up.

But the terrible thing was that Jap mortars over there opened up, too.

The first thing a green man fixes upon in his mind is the noise of these weapons. This was the first time I had ever been surrounded this way by the tight-woven noise of war.

Its constant fabric was rifle fire; this sounded like Bucks County, Pennsylvania, on the first day of the pheasant season, only nearby and not an amusement. Like a knife tearing into the fabric, every once in a while, there would be the short bursts of machine gun fire. The noise of the mortars was awful, a thump which vibrated not just your eardrums, but your entrails as well. Forward we could still hear our aviation— dived bombs fumbling into the jungle, and the laughter of strafing P-39s. And every once in a while the soft, fluttery noise of our artillery shells making a trip. The noise alone was enough to scare a new man, to say nothing of the things which were done by the things which were making the noise.

The Japs had made their calculations perfectly. There were only three or four natural crossings of the river; this was one of them. And so they had set their trap.

They had machine guns all mounted, ready to pour stuff into the jungle bottleneck at the stream's junction with the river. They had snipers scattered on both sides of the river. And they had their mortars all set to lob deadly explosions into the same area. Their plan was to hold their fire and let the enemy get well into the trap before snapping it, and this they had done with too much success.

Apparently the single sniper shot had given the command to the other snipers; when the machine gunners across the river heard all the snipers firing, they let go; and when the Jap mortar batteries farther back heard the machine gun bursts, they in turn opened up.

Had we been infantry, the trap might not have worked. Brave men with rifles and grenades could have wiped out the enemy nests. Captain Rigaud's helplessness was that he could not bring his weapons to bear. Heavy machine guns take some time to be assembled and mounted. In that narrow defile his men, as brave as any, never succeeded in getting more than two guns firing.

As soon as the firing broke out, the men with the machine gun parts rushed together, and regardless of cover put their weapons together. Then the crews felt their way along, trying to find a place where they could both have a little cover and do some harm. As they went they approach-fired, throwing out little fifty-calibre exclamations, as if the guns could say: "Look out, you Japs."

But they never had a chance. The enemy had his guns in position, with nothing to do but aim and squeeze the trigger. And even if the enemy had had no machine guns, his mortar fire had Rigaud's men boxed.

The mortar fire was what was terrifying. Beside it the Japs' sniper fire and even machine gun fire, with its soprano, small-sounding report, seemed a mere botheration. It is hard to think of death as having anything but a deep bass voice. Each roar of mortar certainly seemed to be a word spoken by death.

Having seen Lou Diamond's mortar battery in action, I had a clear picture of what was happening to us. In some small clearing about a half a mile beyond the river, four little tubes, looking like stubby stove pipes, were set up at a high angle on a tripod. Somewhere behind them a Japanese officer stood. A man beside him gave him reports from a telephone or from runners. After each report he would bark out brief orders. A swarm of intelligent little animals would fuss around each tube, changing the angle a hair, turning the aim a trifle. Then the officer would shout to stand by. Some of the animals would step back, one or two at each tube would put their fingers in their ears. Then one, in the attitude of a small boy setting punk to a giant firecracker, would reach out over the mouth of each tube, holding in his hand a thing which looked very much like a miniature aerial bomb, complete with fins. At the order to fire, he would drop the thing, fins first, down the tube. As soon as it struck the bottom there would be a huge thump, and the thing was off on its uncertain flight.

Mortars send their shells in an exceedingly high toss. Consequently their aim is by guess and by God. You will understand this if you have ever seen the job an outfielder has judging a high fly, or if you are an inexpert tennis player and often have been embarrassed by trying to smash a high lob and misjudging it.

That was what made being on the receiving end of mortar fire so terrible: the next thing that those little tubes gave off might land anywhere. We would almost have felt more comfortable if something which could aim was aiming right at us.

When the first bolts of this awful thunder began to fall among Rigaud's men, we hit the ground. We were like earthy insects with some great foot being set down in our midst, and we scurried for little crannies—cavities under the roots of huge trees, little gullies, dead logs. I found a good spot to the left of the trail. It was the combination of a small embankment and a big tree; I grew very affectionate toward the spot; I embraced it. Captain Rigaud, I noticed, took little or no cover. He kept darting back and forth to see what was happening to his men.

What was happening to his men was something terrible. The mortar shells were exploding among them and bleaching some of the bravery out of them. The noise and seeing friends hurt were not things to be dismissed.

The reports were about ten seconds apart, and the shells burst erratically all around us, now fifty yards away, now twenty feet.

And all the while snipers and machine gunners wrote in their nasty punctuation. Our own guns answered from time to time with good, deep, rich sound, but not enough.

We heard one of our guns knocked out. If you have never heard a conversation between two machine guns which are trying to knock each other out, you cannot imagine what a terrible debate it is. At first they talk back and forth equally. Then as in most human arguments, one begins to get the upper hand and finally winds up doing all the talking. That was how it was when our gun was knocked out. It sounded like this:

"Tatatatatatatatatatat," said the Jap gun, in a high Japanese voice.

"Bubububububububububub," said ours, deeply.

"Tatatatatatatatatatatatatat," the Jap insisted.

"Bubububububububububub," said ours.

"Tatatatatatatatat," the Jap said, sure of itself.

"Bubububub. . . . bubub," ours said, uncertainly.

"Tatatatatatatatatatatatatat," the Jap reiterated.

"Bubub." Ours seemed almost to have been convinced.

"Tatatatatatatatat," said the Jap, to clinch the matter.

"Bub," ours said, in pathetic protest.

"Tatatatatatatatat . . . .

"Tatatatatatatatatatatatat."

And then silence. It was awful. (I have heard some conversations in which our guns talked theirs down. Then it is not awful; it makes you cheer.)

I don't believe that this was one of Captain Rigaud's guns. It was a gun belonging to George or Easy Company, and it was manned to the end by a brave man named Sergeant Bauer, about whom I shall tell you a little later.

We could not see the enemy, either on our side of the river or the other. All this hatred was pouring out of jungle too thick to see more than twenty or thirty feet.

This was advantageous, in a way. It meant that the enemy no longer seemed animate. There was no excuse for feelings such as I had had when I picked up the headnet. The firing over there was coming from the enemy as an idea, something easy to hate.

But this invisibility was also unsettling. You might have thought that the jungle itself had grown malevolent, and hated us. The trees were hurling little pellets at us; the vines were slinging great explosions.

But even if we had been able to see the enemy, we could not have done anything to him. We couldn't get our weapons to work. We were helpless. Our men were being killed and wounded. We were trapped, hopelessly trapped.

Individually the marines in that outfit were as brave as any fighters in any army in the world, I am positive; but when fear began to be

Stream Crossing

U.S. Marine
Guadalcanal, B.S.I.P.
Oct. 1942

Sniper

Big One Coming

Walking Wounded

Light ?

Attack

epidemic in that closed-in place, no one was immune. No one could resist it.

The first sign of flight among those men was in their eyes. At first they watched what was going on as calmly as an audience at some play. Then suddenly they were looking around for the nearest exit. They would look at Captain Rigaud's face, looking for some sign that he would order them to retire; or their eyes would dart along the trail back, as they wished they could.

I myself kept looking at Captain Rigaud, to see what he would do with us. His expression had not changed. It had the same look of desperate vigilance that it had worn all along the trail.

The next sign of the growing fear was the way the men started moving around. When a mortar shell would go off nearby, they would scramble away from the vicinity to new cover, as if the thing could explode a second time.

The men began to think that it was time to get away from that whole place.

Any men who were men would have taken flight from that impossible place. Some Japanese might not have, if they had had specific orders to stay there; but they would no longer have been much use to the Emperor. I think even most Japanese would have fled. Certainly Germans would have: they are good fighters: they have the sense to live and fight more advantageously another day. I think it is safe to say that Italians would have fled.

The marines had been deeply enough indoctrinated so that even flight did not wipe out the formulas, and soon the word came whispering back along the line:

"Withdraw."

"Withdraw."

"Withdraw. . . ."

Then they started moving back, slowly at first, then running wildly, scrambling from place of cover to momentary cover.

This was a distressing sight, and though I myself was more than eager to be away from that spot, I had a helpless desire to do something to stop the flight. It seemed wrong. One had heard so much about how the marines kill ten Japs for every man they lose (which is true), of the callousness of the marines (true in a way), and of our endless successes against the Japs (true in sum total). Captain Rigaud had told me that this would probably be an easy job. It sounded so. And yet here were our men running away.

I couldn't do anything about it because I was caught up in the general feeling. It is curious how this feeling communicated itself. Except for the hard knot which is inside some men, courage is largely the desire to show other men that you have it. And so, in a large group, when a majority have somehow signalled to each other a willingness to quit acting, it is very hard indeed not to quit. The only way to avoid it is to be put to shame by a small group of men to whom this acting is life itself, and who refuse to quit; or by a naturally courageous man doing a brave deed.

It was at this moment that Charles Alfred Rigaud, the boy with tired circles under his eyes, showed himself to be a good officer and grown man.

Despite snipers all around us, despite the machine guns and the mortar fire, he stood right up on his feet and shouted out: "Who in Christ's name gave that order?"

This was enough to freeze the men in their tracks. They threw themselves on the ground, in attitudes of defense; they took cover behind trees from both the enemy and the anger of their captain.

Next, by a combination of blistering sarcasm, orders and cajolery, he not only got the men back into position: he got them in a mood to fight again.

"Where do you guys think you're going?" he shouted. And: "Get back in there. . . . Take cover, you. . . . What do you guys do, just invent orders? . . . Listen, it's going to get dark and we got a job to do. . . . You guys make me ashamed. . . ."

But the most telling thing he said was: "Gosh, and they call you marines."

I am certain that all along, Captain Rigaud was just as terrified as the rest of us were, for he was eminently human. And yet his rallying those men was as cool a performance as you can imagine. I could feel my own knees tremble; I could see the rifle shake in the hands of the man nearest me. But I kept quite close to Captain Rigaud and

I could not see a single tremor. If I had, I would have attributed it to anger.

The storm of mortar fire was going on all this while, and so was the lesser fire. Yet now the men, creeping and even running erect, hurried back into the positions they had occupied before. They did this without apparent fear, and yet it was, in effect, the most difficult kind of operation psychologically—a counterattack.

When he had put his men back into position, Captain Rigaud immediately made preparations to get them out in an orderly fashion. There was a big difference between retiring in good order and just running away.

He could see—had seen from the very first mortar explosion—that the position was untenable. Staying there would merely mean losing dozens of men without doing anything to the Japs. He could not get his weapons into play; obviously Whaling's force had not shaken the enemy loose across the river; until he did, this pocket was a place to get killed, nothing more.

Captain Rigaud had talked all his other orders over with his lieutenants, but this decision he made for himself.

"Runner!" he said. "Give me a runner."

One hurried up. Captain Rigaud said: "Give me your message pad."

"It's in my pack, sir," the runner said, and turned his back to the Captain, who reached down into the man's knapsack and pulled out a little yellow pad.

It looked like the kind of pad delivery men carry and make you sign when they bring packages. It had printed-off spaces in which to enter the name of the officer to whom the message was to go, the unit of the sender, his name, the place, time and subject; and then there were several printed lines on which to write the message.

As slowly and carefully as if he were at a desk in Marine Corps headquarters in Washington making out some leisurely requisition, he filled in the blanks.

He addressed the message to Major O'Brien, his regimental commander. He then wrote: "Receiving heavy mortar fire. Unable get machine guns firing. Request permission to withdraw."

He signed it, handed it to the runner and said: "Major O'Brien and hurry."

Then, without waiting for the request for permission to withdraw even to get out of sight, he began to withdraw his men on his own initiative. It was just as well, because Major O'Brien, who had moved up near to George and Easy Companies, had been hit by mortar fire and was a dying man. How he happened to be a dying man and yet not die I shall explain after we have gotten out of this damn valley.

Captain Rigaud did not trust his orders for withdrawal to the whispering system. He moved forward himself, and said quite clearly: "We will withdraw in the same order as we came into the valley: first platoon, third platoon, headquarters, second platoon. The line will double back on itself and form along the trail. Move carefully, keep cover as you fall back. My God, am I ashamed of you guys."

By this time Captain Rigaud had given me enough confidence so that although the awful racket was still going on all around, I could look around and observe what terror does to good young men.

Each man had his little preoccupation. One kept polishing the mud off the stock of his rifle. Another alternately removed and screwed on the cap of his canteen. A third seemed to be counting the buttons on his tunic. Personally I discovered that I was ridiculously tearing very big leaves into very small pieces.

The instinct to crawl into a hole was almost irresistible. One man squeezed himself between the flat, fanning roots of a great tree, and I heard a sergeant whisper contemptuously: "What the hell are you afraid of, that there's bears in these woods?"

Under the influence of fear, some of the men became very systematic over their work. The men who dismantled the machine guns did it with a furious efficiency which was not just haste. They seemed to do the job better than they could have on a drill ground a thousand miles from the enemy.

The men seemed to be impatient with each other. When Captain Rigaud came back from ordering the withdrawal and whispered: "All right, we're not out of here yet: keep a sharp lookout," non-coms and then men passed the order on as if each next man were shirking:

"What you staring at? Keep your eyes peeled," one would whisper testily.

"Okay, dewy-eyes, wake up and keep a lookout," the next would whisper to his neighbor.

"Watch the shrubbery, fathead."

"Dammit, they told us to keep our eyes open: now keep 'em open."

So, variably and angrily, this order was passed.

The beginning of the removal was a slow process. Men at the head of the column fell back on either side of the trail. Occasionally the few who had rifles would fire shots into the jungle in the general direction of snipers' rifle-reports. Gradually the company peeled back, and when they were far enough along, they converged on the trail, in reverse order.

I joined Captain Rigaud again in the headquarters section of the line. As we started up, he turned to whisper to me. He was anxious to defend his men.

"They sure had that mortar fire right on us," he whispered. "Pretty tough for these guys: couldn't get their guns firing out of this pocket. Don't blame 'em for running."

We were going to have quite a wait there on the trail. The machine guns had to be taken apart. Captain Rigaud did not want to move right out without some answer from his commander (Rigaud didn't know Major O'Brien was wounded). And the wounded had to be removed.

As we waited in the trail, the firing was still with us, though it had slackened off somewhat. The men were much calmer now, with the prospect of escaping. Surprisingly to me, they did not whisper to each other about what they had been through, but remained silent, their faces dull and blank. Many sat down, holding their rifles between their knees. Others leaned against trees, and some leaned against each other, back to back, without speaking.

At this time the heroism of the medical corpsmen and bandsmen showed itself. They went into the worst places and began moving the wounded. I joined them because I guess I just thought that was the fastest way to get the hell out of there.

Many of us in these United States have a very distorted idea about how war works. Some of us have had sons or brothers who got into the Army or Navy or Marines (apparently to dodge the draft) and then got into something like the signal corps or quartermasters or intelligence or a medical unit or even a band—and we have had an uneasy feeling that this was somehow not very brave. We have the idea that only those who shoulder a rifle or stand watches on a gun platform or drop in a parachute with a Thompson gun—that only these trigger-pullers are the heroes. The communiqués, which never mention those others, might give us that impression. The citations for medals certainly do. But medals are being given to the wrong people these days.

I said a while back that no men are stronger or braver than the runners, who risk their lives carrying messages alone. I think I must take that back. There is one group who have a little, though not much, edge. They are the wire-stringers. It is their job to carry out a heavy steel spool of copper telephone wire, two in a team, toting the spool on a kind of axle, so it unwinds as they walk. They go everywhere with the spool that a command unit goes, so that the unit may be in telephone communications with its rear base. We in this valley never got in telephone touch because our mission failed, but wire-stringers penetrated the valley, and there were wires all along the trail. After this operation I talked with a private named Leon Stevens who had walked eight miles up and down those awful steeps with a pal and a spool and no protection from enemy bullets. I was exhausted walking less than that and carrying only a pack—but Stevens and the others, exhausted or not, had to stay up most of the night as "trouble-shooters," feeling their way along the wires in the sniper-infested, rainsoaked jungle, looking for a short circuit. Those boys deserve (and almost never get) medals.

But then there is a group who even have a little edge on the wire-stringers. They are the medical units. With the Marines they happen to be Navy medical corpsmen, who are always referred to simply as corpsmen. They are nothing more or less than male nurses. Sounds sissy. But listen to what they do: they go along in every battle, down into every awful valley, unarmed, and they go to the places where the enemy is doing our side most hurt, in order to rescue the wounded. In the face of gunfire, often, they put tags on the clothing of the wounded, telling who it is, what's wrong, and what they've done to relieve the pain. They tell the men who can get themselves off the battlefield where the nearest dressing station behind the lines is; others they carry out or support themselves. They too are liable to have to stay up all night, assisting at an operation. They too deserve medals.

The bandsmen go where the corpsmen go. They are the boys of the regimental bands, the ones you have seen dressed up so fine and marching up the avenue. Only at the front they don't carry their piccolos or trumpets into action: they carry stretchers and syringes of morphine, and they take their chances just like any riflemen. They ought to get some medals.

The group to which I attached myself were wounded in a dreadful way. They had no open wounds; they shed no blood; they seemed merely to have been attacked by some mysterious germ of war that made them groan, hold their sides, limp and stagger. They were shock and blast victims.

There were not enough corpsmen attached to Rigaud's company to assist more than the unconscious and leg-wounded men, so they set these men to helping each other. It was like the blind leading the blind, except that they were also halt.

Some of them were in no condition to walk themselves, to say nothing of helping other men to walk. The group careened along the trail, making hurt noises and not much headway. It was clear that alone they would never reach the advance dressing station, perched upon the ridge from which we had started so long ago. Without any authority to do so, I commandeered three unhurt privates, and we began to half-carry, half-drag the worst of these strange casualties. I took on a boy named Charles Utley.

We must have been a sorry sight, fighting our way along that trail. The rain, and trampling had made it so bad now, that a sound man walking alone would occasionally fall, and in some steep places would have to crawl on hands and knees, pulling himself by exposed roots and leaning bamboo trunks.

We, wounded or laden as we were, slid, crept, walked, wallowed, waded and staggered, like drunken men.

There were places where we had to put the men down, and help them one by one through bottlenecks. The stream crossings were particularly difficult, because the banks were mostly very steep and ragged, and the little spines of coral which we used as ankle-deep bridges were seldom wide enough for more than one set of unsteady legs. The helpers would wade right in, holding up their arms to steady the injured man, who teetered like a tight-rope walker on the coral.

At times a wounded man and the two helping him would all go crashing to the ground, the hurt man groaning and the helpers apologizing bitterly. Sometimes such a three would cut down three others, and the injured and apologetic men would be piled up like cordwood. Now and then a man would faint for a few seconds, and it would be necessary for the whole sickly caravan to wait while some one doused muddy water over his forehead and brought him to.

The walking wounded were magnificent. None of them complained about their own hurts, but inquired politely of each other. There were no whimpers or complaints, only deep-seated groans which expressed real pain.

Our order of march was something like this: First there was a man who kept striking the sides of his befuddled skull with his fists. The second kept his hands over his ears. Then there came two or three men whose legs were badly battered, who behaved like football players with excruciating charley horses; they were able to walk alone, just, but they walked with one leg free and the other stiff, as if it were wooden. The middle of the safari was taken up with the worst wounded and their helpers, and then there were two or three more who could walk—men who generally ached and wished to vomit. In the rear there was a character who shook his head, as if puzzled rather than hurt.

They were a strange-looking band, but they were certainly courageous. I got to like some of them very much in a short time.

One of the worst blast victims, who kept himself conscious only by his guts, was the man I was with, Utley. He had a caved-in chest, and one of his legs was bruised almost beyond use.

Back home in his dress blues, Charles Utley would have been handsome; but here he was a mess. His blond hair, longer than usual for a marine, was tousled and sweaty—he had left his helmet behind. There were streaks on his face of sweat and mud. His shirt was open down the front and wet down the back.

Part of the time we had to carry him, part of the time he could, by concentrating hard, drag his feet along while I and another supported him. We tried every means of locomotion, to make his way easy. For a while we carried him seated on two rifles. We tried making a stretcher out of the rifles and a poncho, but he was more comfortable standing up. We made a seat of our hands, until we couldn't carry him any more, and kept falling down. Most of the time, though, we took his arms over our shoulders and dragged him along between us, with occasional brave help or accidental hindrance from him.

Before we had gone very far, we were met in the trail by a corpsman, who, seeing what pain Utley was in, got out a little morphine syringe and injected ease into him. You can judge how he felt when you know that the prick of the needle made this brave lad faint away. It was easy to bring him round by wetting my handkerchief from my canteen and cooling his forehead.

As we moved painfully along, his head lolled from side to side. He would look in the face of the other helper and in mine and try an occasional smile. And gradually he groaned less and tried a few words, which proved in the end to be consecutive, and quite a story.

"Bauer," he said, when he had got his tongue under control.

I thought he was trying to tell us his name, because he had no corpsman's tag and I didn't know then that his name was Utley.

"Bauer," he said again a little farther on.

"Okay, Mac," the other helper said, "just take it easy."

He said it a third time, when we were trying to get him across a stream: "Bauer."

We had a little difficulty on the other side of the stream, and I said:

"All right, Bauer, just sit down here while we get up where we can pull you up."

His sleepy-looking eyes opened quite wide, and he tried to look around. "Bauer all right?" he asked.

He was talking rather thickly, and we thought perhaps his mind was rambling a little. But he came back to the same question when we had started moving again.

"Bauer all right?"

"Is Bauer your name?" I asked.

"Name's Utley," he said. "Charles Utley. Bauer all right?"

"Who in hell is this Bauer?" the other helper asked.

"Don't you know'm? Bauer. He all right?"

"Yeah, he's fine, Mac. He's all right," the other helper said. He had decided, and I agreed, that it was better to put his mind at rest.

But Utley wasn't satisfied. He frowned for quite a distance, then he said: "You sure?"

"Sure what, Mac?"

"He's all right. Bauer. He here?"

We asked ahead and we asked behind: "Any of you guys Bauer? You know where he is?"

Bauer was not with us. One of the men with a bad leg said: "Bauer he won't never come out."

We struggled along for almost two hundred yards, and Utley was silent. I thought he had forgotten all about what he had been talking about, until he said:

"Shouldn't've gone back. He never should've."

We knew he was talking about the same man.

"Back where, Utley?" I asked.

"Gun. No use. Never should've gone back."

"Why not?" I was interested in Bauer now.

"All finished. We were all knocked round. Gun was jammed. Bauer he was bad hurt. Japs knew where we were, goddam bastards."

Quite a bit farther along, after we had sat Utley down to rest beside the stream, and I had washed his face off, and he seemed much better, I said: "Now, do you think you could tell me exactly what happened, about Bauer I mean?"

"Sure," he said. "You know him?"

"No, never seen him."

"Rugged. Nice guy, awful nice guy. Never should've gone back to that gun."

"Would you start right at the beginning?"

"Sure. We had this gun, see. Bauer, he was our boss. He's a sergeant, rugged kind of guy. He told us they had said to get the gun set up beside the river. No use to do it from the beginning, see, cause we couldn't register on the Japs, couldn't even see 'em, say nothing of killing 'em. Trouble is they knew right where we were at, on account of that was the good place to cross the river. No use to the whole thing from the beginning."

The parade of staggering men began to move again, and as Utley did not offer right away to continue his story, I didn't press him, since it probably wasn't too good for him to think and talk too much. There was no stopping him thinking about Bauer, though, and a bit farther on he said: "He shouldn't have gone back. Who let him go back anyway?"

After another short rest, I asked him to go on about the gun and so forth.

"No use to the damn thing," he said. "We no more'n begun to approach-fire, see, when the Japs put it right on us and we couldn't see where the hell they was at. We tried the best we could but it wasn't much use to it. They had us and we didn't have them not in the least. Then this grenade or mortar or some goddam thing it hit us. Oh gee, that was something bad. All white, see, it made your eyes go. And a hell of a noise like I never heard and I hope to die I never do again. Well see, it knocked us around like a bunch of damn alley pins."

"Was that when you got yours?"

"Yeah, that's what done this to me. Geez, I never felt like this before at all, what you guess it could be from, like this? No bullets, no blood. Just around my chest it's so hard to breathe. Well anyway, Bauer he was dizzy just like all the rest of us and apparently no scratches, just gaga like us. We all crawled back over a hump kind of a place and left our machine gun turned over but looked like it was okay down there."

This was apparently the gun we had heard in unsuccessful debate with the Japanese gun.

"Bauer, the damn fool, I shouldn't say that, you wouldn't find a better man, he lay there hurt like the rest of us behind this mound but then he got up and said: 'I'll show those sonsabitches,' and ran right on down and he was just turning the gun right-side to when another one of those big damn things came and landed right behind him, oh jiminy, it was awful. You see we could see his back was all blood and I guess he was dead. We moved back then because it doesn't rain twice but it rains three times and we knew there'd be another of those things over with everybody's name on it. That's all it was."

We were silent for a long time. Now that the morphine had had time to ease his pain, Utley's body was stronger just as his mind was clearer. But from then on, except for little remarks about how he could help us help him, he only said:

"He shouldn't've gone back. Why in the hell did he have to go on back?"

The farther we went, the harder the going seemed to be. We all became tired, and the hurt men slowed down considerably. There were some steep places where we had to sit Utley down in the mud, and slide him down ten feet to the stream; in other places, uphill, we had to form a chain of hands and work him up very slowly. It was almost dark by the time we had reached the thin place, and by the time we had negotiated the last, open steep, it was hard to tell the difference between the wounded men and the bearers.

Heaven, if it looks anything like the view that greeted us when we regained the top of the ridge, will be a welcome sight. I have never seen anything so beautiful. It was dusk. The air had gone immaculately clean, and all that had been so soft and mysterious in the morning was now hard purple fact. Florida, Tulagi and Savo stood up out of the crystalline sea positively, and the heights of Point Esperance, uncovered now, were perfectly defined. Point Cruz, Lunga Point, every feature of the landscape was clean and definite—an assurance of reality. I guess that is why the scene seemed so beautiful: it was so real, it was a quiet wakening after a bad dream.

The advance dressing station was set up on the military crest at just about the point where we had gone down into the valley. It consisted merely of a collection of equipment—stretchers, boxes of medicines, bandages, chlorine to purify water, operating gear. Four stretchers had been raised up on their ends and leaned against each other, and a poncho had been thrown over the top, as a crude little tent. As hospitals go, this was basic.

The commanding officer, to whom we turned over the wounded, was Lieutenant Commander William W. New, U.S.N.R., a kind of young military David Harum. I had met him back in camp the night before we left, and had liked him immensely. He had come up to Colonel Sims's tent and sat down at the root of a tree, with a cigar in his mouth, silent for a long time. Then, without removing the cigar, he had asked: "Reckon we can get any more stretcher bearers for out there?" Colonel Sims had said he thought not. Doc New said that anyone who thought two men were enough for a stretcher was very old-fashioned; that in this country there were places where six wouldn't be too many. Colonel Sims said we would just have to do the best we could; whereupon Doc New changed the subject.

The first thing Doc New did when he reached his bivouac on the battlefield was to take things into his hands in a most unusual way. He sent a dispatch to divisional headquarters: "Need additional stretchers and one hundred bearers." Of course the request was countermanded as soon as regimental command learned about it. But Doc New was quite right, from the medical if not from the military point of view: there simply were not enough men to help the wounded off the field.

Doc New has a round face, a bristly mustache, and teeth which are not so much repaired as illuminated with gold. He comes from Guthrie, Oklahoma, and he is very careful with his language. When he gets excited, he rolls off such exclamations as "Dadgummitding-whiz." The morning before we went out into the field, he pressed three cigars on me, and every time we met on the battlefield he offered me another—and through all the rain and mud and work he kept his supply quite dry.

When we turned our decrepit band over to him, Doc New took up his activity as if possessed. He hurried from man to man, and if they wore no tags, he asked abruptly what was wrong and what had been done for them. He tagged them and sorted them and questioned them and put them on stretchers and took their pulse and gave them a drink and threw ponchos over them, and altogether was so busy with them that they looked as if they might almost prefer to be back in the valley. But under his firm hand they soon felt much better.

A ghost walked up to me on that ridge—or at least I thought it was one. It was Captain Rigaud. I had no idea that he would be out ahead of me.

"What became of you?" he asked. "I looked all over for you."

I told him that I had come out with some of the wounded, and said that I was sorry if I caused him any worry. He hadn't been around when I left Company H, and I had asked some of the headquarters group to tell him what I was doing; evidently they forgot. "But how did you beat me out?" I asked. "I thought I was way ahead of you."

"We took a shortcut. We came up over there." He pointed along the ridge. They had come up at the very spot where they had decided not to go down in the morning because of the steepness. A precipice would have been negotiable as an exit from the valley.

Captain Rigaud tried to apologize for his men again: "The Japs sure had their mortars right on," he said. "There was nothing those fellows with the guns could do."

"Too bad we didn't have Lou Diamond to send some mortar fire back at them," I said.

"You know Lou?" he said.

I told him I had seen Lou in action, and that a couple of the men had told me that he was in Company H.

"Yeah," he said, "if we'd had Lou, it would have been a different story." Then after a pause he said: "What're you going to do now? You going back to the States?"

"Not tonight," I said. "But soon, I guess."

"What I'd give to be you," he said.

After what I had seen him do in the valley that afternoon, in the face of fear in his ranks and in his own heart, I would have given something to be Captain Rigaud, homesickness and all.

I remembered Bauer, so I went over to one of Doc New's corpsmen and asked if anyone had reported him. The corpsman said a group had already gone down into the valley to look for him.

There were both corpsmen and bandsmen in the group. They had stood on the ridge all afternoon and heard the music in that valley, so they knew what they were going into.

It was pitch dark when those heroic boys found Bauer. They were in territory, remember, where snipers had been all around, and where, if they betrayed themselves by the slightest sound, they would have mortar fire pouring down on them.

They found Bauer lying just about where Utley and the others had last seen him. He had dragged himself away from the gun a bit into a place of partial cover.

One of the bandsmen whispered: "How you feel, Mac?"

Bauer whispered: "I think I can make it."

The men fashioned a crude stretcher out of two rifles and a poncho, and started out. Bauer was in bad shape. He was conscious, but that was about all. He seemed very uncomfortable lying flat on the poncho, and during one of the rests he struggled to sit up. Two of the boys reached down to help him, and one of them, Sergeant Lewis Isaak, a clarinetist, found out the nature of Bauer's wound—by putting his hand right in the middle of it. It was a big, soft, warm, wet place in the man's back, and in the dark it gave Isaak the shivers. Bauer groaned a little when Isaak put his hand in the place.

Now that the wound was located, one of the corpsmen put a crude dressing on it. He just felt for the extent of it, cleaned it off as best he could, and planked a big flat dressing, damn near as big as a bedsheet, over it. He and another gave Bauer two shots of morphine.

The only way the group could find their way was to follow, hand over hand, a telephone wire which some wirestringer had carried into that hot valley. One stayed out in front, tracing the wire and whispering directions. One man took each corner of the stretcher. In the darkness they had a terrible time making any headway. Besides all the things we had had to contend with earlier in the day, they now were carrying a dying man, and they could not see where. They would bump into trees and stumble over roots. It took several seconds to find footing for each step. The load, the worry and the darkness wore them out fast, and they had to stop for frequent rests.

There happened to be two boys named Cox in the gang carrying Bauer, and nobody, not even the two Coxes, knew that there were two Coxes. That led to some trouble.

One of them was Private Charles Cox, a very tall southern boy, slightly deaf but nevertheless a bass horn player in the regimental band. He had been working on some other wounded all day, and he was practically a casualty, he was so tired.

When they came to one of their resting places and put Bauer down, Private Charles Cox announced in a whisper that he was so durn tired he was going to have to snatch a nap; and for goodness sakes to wake him up when they started up again. A couple of the others who knew him whispered okay.

He picked himself a rootless hollow, flopped down, put his hands back of his head, and turned off his consciousness like an electric light.

About ten minutes later the gang decided to move on. Charles Cox had pulled himself away from the rest, and the ones who had promised to wake him did not know exactly where he was. So Isaak spoke out softly: "Cox! Come on, Cox, we're moving."

"I'm here," said the Cox who was not Charles, "I'm all ready."

The bearers raised Bauer and went along. Charles Cox went right on sleeping.

He woke up about midnight. It took him a couple of seconds to realize where he was, and when he did, his first thought was to curse the supposed pals who had failed to waken him.

But then he left off cursing them because he realized what a hell of a mess he was in. He was alone in a jungle full of Japs. He had no rifle because of the work he was doing. He had got separated from the wire, which was his only chance of finding his way out in the dark. He decided there was nothing to do but sit tight and hope for the best in the morning.

Needless to say, Charles Cox did not fall asleep again that night, even though a few hours before he had been so tired he could hardly hold his head up. Sounds grew big beyond proportion, until the rubbing together of two branches seemed like whole regiments crashing through the bush.

As soon as light began to show the pattern of branches and leaves overhead, he started to move stealthily back to friendly country. After day had really broken, he found the trail and walked along it. He had turned around so much that he was not certain he was going in the right direction.

At one point he drew sniper fire. He hit the ground and crawled for cover. Before he showed up again among the friends who had not made sure of his being awake, he crawled, slid, hid, walked and ran about eight frightened miles.

After they moved on and left the sleeping Cox, the corpsmen and bandsmen came to a steep place where they found that they could not handle Bauer without help; and so about three men went up to get fresh carriers.

Sergeant Isaak and one or two others stayed with the wounded man. Isaak tried to soothe his pain and make things easy for him in the only ways he could imagine. He held Bauer's head and spoke to him softly.

Men who are wounded do not talk rhetorically; famous last words are usually edited after the fact. Bauer's sentences were simple requests: "Help me sit up, will you please, oh God my stomach . . ."

Then when he was up he hurt more than ever, so he said: "No, no, I've got to lie down, do it slowly."

Then Bauer whispered: "Say fellows, would you help me to take a crap? My stomach hurts, if I could just take a crap."

They took his pants down, propped him up and held him in such a way that he could do what he wanted. Afterwards he felt a little better. He leaned back seeming to be exhausted.

For a few moments his head tossed quickly from side to side. Then he said very softly: "I wish I could sleep."

The wish was fulfilled: he dropped off in apparent peace. He gave a few short breaths and then just stopped breathing. When the others got back, a corpsman examined him, and pronounced Sergeant Bauer, who had not been satisfied to stay under cover when there was a machine gun to be fired, dead.

I never did find out exactly how many men were killed, and how many wounded in that valley. It would have been hard to be statistical about that little incident. But I do know that one less died than would otherwise have, if Doc New hadn't been mighty handy in an emergency.

This one was Major O'Brien, Captain Rigaud's Battalion commander—the one to whom the Captain had addressed his request for permission to withdraw.

The Major had been hurt by the same mortar fire as we had encountered. He was carried out of the valley by corpsmen and was turned over to Doc New at his dressing station on top of the ridge.

At the time when Doc New first examined him, the Major was a dying man. He was in absolute shock. He was gray as ashes in the face. His hands were cold. You could not feel his pulse.

He had suffered a bad flesh wound from mortar shrapnel above his left knee, and he had another shrapnel wound in his right hand. He had obviously lost a great deal of blood. Doc New realized that plasma and lots of it was all that could save this man. Administering plasma there, with mud for an operating table and filth and Japs all around, was a ticklish job.

Doc New had to maintain blackout. He had also to try to keep the man warm, to help him come out of shock. To serve both these ends, most of his corpsmen gave up what little shelter they had against the cold and damp night, their ponchos. Working feverishly, interposing such expressions as "Dadgummit" and "Gollydingwhiz," he covered first the wounded man, then his own head and shoulders, with ponchos. I am not positive that Doc New ever took his cigar out of his mouth.

With a flashlight in one hand and a transfusion needle in the other, with a dentist for an assistant and a chaplain for a nurse, he got the Major ready to take some plasma. Before the first unit of 250 cc. was all in, the patient came out of his coma. By the time the second was in, he was able to speak. By morning he was able to talk to his C.P. on a field phone, stand the ride on a stretcher down to the beach road, and sit up in a jeep on the way back to the hospital.

When I got back to Colonel Sims's command post, my friends offered me a ready-made foxhole. It was already nearly dark, and all along the ridge the marines, who looked like strangely animated dead men, were wrapping themselves in ponchos, stretching themselves out stiff in their gravelike holes, and doing everything by way of last rites except to scoop the dirt in over themselves. My clothes were soaked and caked with mud, the Japs were much closer than they had been during the first, sleepless night, and artillery fire was just as frequent—but this time I dropped off within five minutes and slept dreamlessly all night long.

I was wakened by the first of an artillery barrage and a responding cry from an exultant marine: "Aha! Reveille, you lousy Japs!"

The sunrise that morning, after the slop and terror of the day before, was one of the most beautiful things a lot of marines had ever seen. One named Bill said: "Any one who can't see beauty in that doesn't deserve to live. My mother would like to see that. 'Dear Mom: You should've seen the sunrise this morning. . . .' "

A few of us felt that we would rather die than start that day without some hot coffee. We scoured around for some dry wood and finally, at the upper edge of a coral precipice, found some little bushes that had been a season dead and weathered. We broke twigs up into tiny faggots about twice the size of matches. We lit up and found to our delight that the twigs burned with a light blue haze, which was not a betrayal. One fellow who had not helped us gather the twigs kept putting his canteen cup right over the best part of the fire, until one of the others snapped at him: "Didn't you never hear of that old American custom, no work no eat? Scram, Mac."

After our coffee, feeling much less decrepit, we went out onto the utmost ridge before the valley of the Matanikau. It stuck out over and into the jungle like a promontory intruding on some dark sea.

There were lookout posts stationed on this ridge, and so we could see all there was to be seen of that morning's action. Operations, we found, proceeded according to plan—the formal way of saying "with moderate but unspectacular success."

At 8:50 we saw two men, then a large group, move up onto the ridge on the other side of the river which lay nearest the beach. One of this group, we could see through field glasses, peeled out yellow and black semaphore flags and signalled: "Have taken hill. Moving down to beach."

Across from us, on higher ridges not so close to the shore, we saw marines spread out white cloth panels to show our aviation where not to bomb. Our planes spread-eagled out beyond, making the valleys sound and resound.

I heard a marine chanting: "All *right,* ladies and gent'men, step right up and take a peek. Ten cents a look, it's wonderful, it's romantic. Don't miss it. Only ten cents. . . ."

There was quite a line of marines waiting to look through this man's observation telescope set up on a tripod at the front edge of a foxhole. Of course they weren't paying dimes to look through it, but each man got down on his belly in the foxhole, squinted, drew in his breath, muttered an exclamation of pleasure, then yielded up the scope. Curious, I took my place in the line.

I saw first a blurred circle. When I had focussed, I saw that the scope was trained on the sandspit running across the mouth of the Matanikau. On the spit, in frozen attitudes of prostrate haste, were a whole bunch of dead bodies. It was easy to see by the wrapped leggings that they were Jap bodies.

A few hours later I found out why those bodies were there. They were testimony to the bitterest clash of the whole three-day battle. On my way back into camp I went to the river mouth, and as I looked at Japanese bodies curled in foxholes and sprawled on the spit—marine bodies had already been removed—I felt a tug at my sleeve and a bitter voice saying: "We meet again." The voice belonged to a captain of the Raiders. He told me what had happened. Apparently Edson had had trouble getting rid of the company on his side of the river, and so called on the men who do or die in the worst jams in Guadal, the Raiders. During the previous night, the Japs had decided to make a break for the spit, their only avenue of escape. They mounted a terrifying attack. About half the Japs started screaming and shouting, while the other half advanced silently and slipped into foxholes with the marines, who had no way of knowing whether their silent visitors were advancing enemy or retreating friends. But in the close-in knife work which followed, the marines evidently got the best of it, to judge by the number of Jap bodies in the holes. Of those who broke through, most were apparently cut down on the spit. There were seventy Jap bodies in the vicinity, members of the Second Company of the Fourth Regiment of the Sendai Division, big Japs in brand new uniforms, carrying brand new packs containing brand new spare socks and brand new rice bags. The Raiders lost thirteen dead and had twenty-seven wounded.

After my turn at the scope, I rejoined some of Sims's headquarters group who were out on that ridge. One of them told me he had just seen a flare near the beach of the color and type which meant: "No assistance needed." Apparently things were in hand.

Five minutes later a signalman appeared on the hill near the beach and semaphored: "Fox Company has reached the beach."

About fifteen minutes after that two or three wild pigs, such as are to be found on Guadal, were apparently killed in or near the little collection of palm-leaf huts that used to be Matanikau Village, for we heard the most blood-chilling screams, such as you hear at an abattoir. One of the marines chilled my blood a few extra degrees by remarking calmly: "Might be boars screaming just like men. On the other hand, might be men screaming something like pigs."

The action was drawing to a close. I heard a command go out: "Whaling group reorganize and withdraw by beach road at once." And a few minutes later this command went out to Puller, who was leading the deepest penetration of Sims's men: "Execute reconnaissance with your battalion along coast toward Kokombona. Do not become involved in large action. Be prepared to withdraw on order by beach road."

Before the battle was over and the lines dissolved and trickled back into camp, I wanted to see Captain Rigaud again. I inquired around and learned that his bivouac was not far from Colonel Sims's.

His bivouac lay in a kind of amphitheater cupped between two fingers of a ridge. The men were scattered around over an area of about two hundred yards square—sitting on the edges of their side-hill foxholes, holding their shoes in hand and scraping the mud off, cleaning small arms, taking off their shirts and spreading them out to dry.

The air this morning was bland, and in Rigaud's amphitheater it seemed especially soft. The sun beat down and warmed those marines and melted away the cold thing that had settled hard inside them the afternoon before. Now, with their guessing that the battle was almost over, they relaxed in the warmth, and you could hear throaty laughs, the short explosions that follow dirty jokes, bouncing around the bivouac.

Captain Rigaud was sitting near a radio post. He did not seem to be doing anything at the moment when I came up, just looking out between the grassy fingers over Lunga Point, with its exact fringe of bright green palm, on over the sky-blue sea toward the sea-blue sky. He jumped a little when I spoke to him.

"Oh hello," he said. "You look terrible."

"Thank you. So do you."

I didn't know then about me, but he certainly was a mess. His third morning of beard had begun to put a dark cross-hatch on his pale cheeks and chin. His uniform was caked with mud. The circles under his eyes were no smaller and no less tired. His slender violinist's hands were dirty.

He at once began apologizing for the third time for what his men had done. "The Japs sure had us located, didn't they? That mortar fire was right on. No way of telling where it was coming from right in that pocket there."

I couldn't say what I wanted to, so I just asked what kind of mortars the Japs used, and he said the firing down there had come, most probably, from mortars very much like our own 81-mm. Stokes-Brandt. I sat down on the hillside, and two or three of Rigaud's lieutenants meandered over and sat down too, and for a while I asked some questions and they gave the answers on some technical things.

Then I asked what the orders were for Company H that morning.

"We're just supposed to stand by for now, Captain Rigaud said. "I expect we'll have to go in to do some cleaning up sooner or later. Guess there's only one thing we can bank on: we aren't going home."

I asked how the casualties had been in the Company in the valley.

"We don't really know yet. Not too bad, I hope." I couldn't tell whether to believe his words or his face.

"Oh say," I said, "I took three of your men out to help with some hurt fellows. I should have asked your permission. I'm sorry."

All he said was: "Good. That's three more."

I asked Captain Rigaud how the whole three day battle seemed to have shaped up.

"Not too good," he said. "Just a half-way success, I guess. The Japs seem to have pulled out last night, from what I hear. I don't think we caught as many as we wanted to." I learned later that two hundred Jap bodies were found on the field. The Japs had evidently pulled out in quite a hurry, because they left packs and other equipment behind. The Marines lost sixty dead—their worst casualties in any single operation on Guadal up to that time.

"We didn't move fast enough," one of the lieutenants said.

"We got to be better on communications," another said. "Jeez, the way we got scared by G and E Companies yesterday."

"I guess you got a lousy impression of the way us guys operate," one of them said to me. "We're not the bums of the world, really."

I wanted to tell Captain Rigaud how much I admired him and those bums of his, but I just said: "Anything I can do for any of you when I get back?"

"Oh no thanks," Captain Rigaud said. "I guess we'll be coming back in this afternoon or tomorrow anyhow."

"No," I said. "I mean when I get back to the States."

The men answered after a pause.

"Say, eat me a piece of blueberry pie, would you?" one said.

"I wonder if you'd give my mother a telephone call in Bronxville," another said. "From New York it's only about thirty cents."

I turned to Captain Rigaud. "Anything for you, Captain?"

"You going to New York?" he asked.

"Yes."

"Well, if you go through a place called Oriskany Falls, wish you'd tell my folks you saw me."

I said I would have to say more than that.

"And then when you get to New York," he said, "I want you to take a hot bath, in a bath tub, long one, about twenty minutes. Then put on a soft white shirt, with a good-looking tie, and a double-breasted blue suit. And then go out and—what's a good bar in New York?"

"Oh, I don't know, there are lots."

"Well, go to one of them that's good and walk up to the bar and order two Tom Collinses, tall ones. One is for you and one belongs to Captain Charles Rigaud. I don't care how you drink yours, gulp it for all I care; but Captain Rigaud's drink, sip it, take a half an hour if you got to. And you may as well mumble something formal, like a toast. Drink a toast to Company H. If they aren't on Guadal, they'll be way the hell and gone out somewhere. Yeah, that's a good idea. Do that."